IRA Misfortune 101

Learn the best kept secrets in the financial world today!

If you are investing in a Retirement Account and counting on these funds to help secure your future retirement years, you need to read this book!

Learn how to turn your *MISFORTUNE* into a REAL FORTUNE!

Tim H Cooper, CRFA®

IRA Misfortune 101

This publication is designed to provide accurate and authoritative information on the subject of Individual Retirement Accounts. However, it is sold with the understanding that neither the Author or the Publisher is engaged in rendering legal, accounting, financial or other professional services by publishing this book. As each individual situation is unique, specific questions about your personal finances should be addressed to a qualified professional to ensure that the situation has been evaluated carefully and appropriately. The Author and Publisher specifically disclaim and liability, loss or risk which is incurred as a consequence, directly, or indirectly, of the use and application of contents of this work.

The CRFA® certification mark is owned by The Society of Certified Retirement Financial Advisors.

Order this book online at www.trafford.com
or email orders@trafford.com

Most Trafford titles are also available at major online book retailers.

Editors: Dianne Garrett and Glenda S. Cooper

Note for Librarians: A cataloguing record for this book is available from Library and Archives Canada at www.collectionscanada.ca/amicus/index-e.html

Printed in Victoria, BC, Canada.

ISBN: 978-1-4269-1595-6 (sc)
ISBN: 978-1-4269-1596-3 (hc)

Library of Congress Control Number: 2009935849

Our mission is to efficiently provide the world's finest, most comprehensive book publishing service, enabling every author to experience success. To find out how to publish your book, your way, and have it available worldwide, visit us online at www.trafford.com

Trafford rev. 12/07/2009

www.trafford.com

North America & international
toll-free: 1 888 232 4444 (USA & Canada)
phone: 250 383 6864 ♦ fax: 812 355 4082

IRA: Individual Retirement Account.
Financial Instrument used to help offset living expenses during the retirement phase of an individual's life. These retirement accounts can be in various forms:: Traditional, Roth, 403 (b), 401 (k), SEP, Solo K, 457, Keogh, Simple). All designated to give the same result. HOWEVER, What is best for you can be defined differently by so many variables.

MISFORTUNE: An incident of bad luck, mischance or mishap. In today's financial market we have all experienced: *MISFORTUNE.*

However, there are many options available to the average investor that are not offered by all custodial institutions. Many financial institutions are not advising their clients about certain situations which can occur.

In *IRA MISFORTUNE 101,* we review various unique situations and how there are vast options available for those who are preparing to retire, who are already retired or those who have set goals for their retirement years.

With *IRA Misfortune 101* we help explain how you can be more in control of your investments, where you can decide how and when these funds are designated, invested and held.

Your financial structure is unique to you and no different than any other aspect of your life which you control. You decide what color you paint your house. Shouldn't you be able to do the same for your investment dollars?

Are you in *CONTROL?*

Start learning today on how to turn your

MISFORTUNE

into a

REAL FORTUNE!

IRA Misfortune 101

Contents

Introduction

This book is designed for individuals and their beneficiaries who are already adding contributions to a retirement plan, retired or retiring shortly. You probably would have expected your financial advisor or accountant to share the information in this book with you, however 25 years of experience has exposed some misinformation at many levels. The arena of handling your IRA or other retirement accounts, other than how to invest it, is not widely understood because it's complex.

Think about your IRA (or retirement plan) as if it were your home. You already know how to select furniture, (fund your IRA, pick investments) for the house. Fewer people understand how to construct the house (maximizing the efficiency of the IRA), move it from one town to another (correct rollover transactions), or make structural changes to the house (investment changes or Roth conversions). This book explains these issues regarding:

1.Movement of your money from your company once you retire.

2.Managing of the account once it is in your own name:

    a. Taking necessary distributions

    b. Ways to reduce income tax on distributions

    c. Ways to get maximum tax deferral

    d. Protection from creditors.

    e. Misinformed advisor direction

    f. Alternative IRA Investment Choices

    g. Beneficiary Issues

    h. Trusts as IRA Beneficiary

3.   Establishing the account to have greatest value to heirs (it's doubtful that you will spend every last dime of your IRA, when maybe it should be a high consideration to spend that money first since it's plagued with complicated tax issues for you and your heirs). Also, it's most likely they will, or have been, directed improperly.

4.   You have volunteered to make contributions to a retirement account (403(b), 401(k), IRA, Solo (k), SEP, Keogh plans) for years. The interesting thing is many of you spent 18 seconds making the decision to make these contributions with no study of the complication and confusion these plans can have on getting your money, investing your money, withdrawing your money, giving this money to your heirs or maybe your favorite charity . Maybe you have discovered the IRA is not yours. Well your right, it's not until you cash out. Actually, the IRS and Department of Labor is allowing you to be the trustee of the IRA Trust. How do you rate yourself? Would I hire you to make decisions for my IRA?

Today I am blessed to have spent over 25 years in this business, I have met thousands of people, have been associated with many financial institutions, broker dealers, insurance companies, first class financial advisors, and there is very little time spent on issues raised in this book.

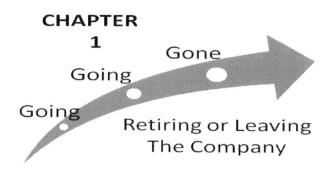

CHAPTER 1

Retiring or Leaving The Company

Whether you are moving towards an independent lifestyle, changing jobs, or an employment termination, you need to know what to do with your employer sponsored retirement plan before your leave. Once you leave a job for whatever reason, you may request to:

- Rollover the money into an IRA.
- Take the lump sum and pay the income tax and any IRS enforced penalties.
- Leave the money at the company if the company offers that as an option.
- Rollover the money into your new employer's plan, if that plan accepts rollovers.
- Transfer the money to your favorite charity

Realize that the above are options offered by the IRS. However, your employer's retirement plan rules may be more restrictive, and if so, there may be limited options for you. For example, if you have a pension plan that offers payout options over your lifetime, or jointly over the lifetimes of you and your spouse, but there is no option to rollover a lump sum to an IRA, the rollover option isn't available to you. In other words, the "summary plan document" is your rule book. You may want to get a copy of that now and have your financial advisor review it so that you know what options you have. Our experience has shown that most individuals sign up for a company retirement plan, and choose investment options for these accounts in just a few seconds, spending no time evaluating evidence to support their reasons for employing their money in tax deferred accounts.

What is a Rollover?

Rollover means to move money from a retirement plan such as a 401(k), 403b (tax sheltered annuity), or 457 (municipal deferred compensation) into an IRA or other plan. If you receive a payout from your employer-sponsored retirement plan, a rollover IRA could be to your advantage. You would continue to receive the tax-deferred status of your retirement savings and would avoid penalties.

There are three reasons that rollovers are favored over other options:

- You have virtually unlimited investment selections. Unlike your employer's plan which may have ten, twenty or maybe fifty investment options. With an IRA, you can choose any stock, mutual fund, money market, certificate of deposit, and a host of other investments.

- Company plans often can restrict choices for non-spouse beneficiaries. Specifically, they may not be able to stretch IRA distributions over their lifetime. The concept behind a "Stretch IRA" is that the IRA defers taxes and allows the funds to potentially grow longer and larger in a tax-deferred environment.

- There are special retirement accounts that can allow your IRA to buy real estate, land, vacation properties, commercial properties, loan your IRA money to others, buy a business and much more. We will discuss the options later in book.

One reason to leave your retirement plan with your company (if permitted) is to afford continued coverage by ERISA protecting it from creditors. However, under the new Bankruptcy Abuse Prevention and Consumer Protection Act of 2005, the creditor protection will follow the money if it is rolled into an IRA and not co-mingled with other IRA money from annual contributions. For example: Your IRA is insured from creditors up to $1,000,000. I suggest a review of your state statutes on filing bankruptcy when you have creditors.

Combining Retirement Accounts:

The rollover IRA is usually funded by the eligible distributions from a company-sponsored retirement plan. These distributions can be combined with your existing IRA(s) or placed into a separate IRA, but see the new creditor protection rule mentioned above. In fact, the IRS permits these funds to be combined with other types of retirement accounts. For example, say you have been self employed and you have a one-person profit sharing plan (maybe a Keogh plan), you could rollover the employer-plan assets into your profit sharing plan. Or, if you have a second job and that employer has a 403(b) plan and also accepts rollover contributions, you could rollover your 401 (k) balance into that 403(b) plan.

Completing your Rollover:

When it's time to retire, you have a few options on moving the money from your employer's plan.

Direct Rollover: Your employer can directly rollover your retirement plan payout into a Rollover IRA and you will avoid the 20% IRS withholding tax. This is exactly what you should do by providing your employer the name, address and account number of your new Rollover IRA custodian. For example, you give your employer instructions to send your retirement account to Big Street Securities, account #AOH-8889999. Funds are sent directly to the IRA account and you never touch them. This is the preferred method of moving retirement funds.

Payout by Check: If your employer hands you a check for your retirement funds, the employer must withhold 20% for potential taxes. You can avoid the 20% IRS withholding tax on a payout by check from your employer if you deposit the check plus 20% into a rollover IRA within 60 days. In order to complete the tax free rollover, you now have 80% of your IRA rollover in your hand, and you must take the other 20% out of your pocket so that you have a completely tax free rollover (you will get the 20% income tax withheld as a refund after you file your tax return). This payment option may require you to take money out of your pocket to complete your rollover.

Taking a lump sum distribution: This option will trigger ordinary income tax on the distribution, most likely at the top of your current tax bracket. It is also possible that some of this distribution will be pushed into the next higher tax bracket. If you are under age 59 ½ you will pay an additional 10% early withdrawal tax. However, there may be reasons to take a taxable distribution. If you are set on buying a $300,000 boat and spending the rest of your life floating about the globe, then you should discuss your plan with a qualified advisor. The advisor may choose to use a scientific model to review several strategies to help you minimize the tax and maximize the benefit. However, if you can avoid using these funds and don't mind deferring happiness, this money may bring today, with a bit of luck, this nest egg will be there when you mature in age!

Ten Year Averaging

What is Qualified Lump Sum Distribution for Ten Year Averaging?

It is the distribution or payment in one tax year of a plan participant's entire balance from all of an employer's qualified plans of one kind (for example, pension, profit-sharing, or stock bonus plans) in which the participant had funds. The participant's entire balance does not include deductible voluntary employer contributions or certain forfeited amounts

The participant must have been **born before January 2, 1936.**

If you are a plan beneficiary to a taxpayer whose date of birth was before January 2,1936, you may qualify for ten year averaging on a lump sum distribution. Ten year averaging allows up to 50% of the total distribution to be tax free and the balance will be subject to very low tax rates as described.

IRA Misfortune 101

Distributions upon death of the plan participant. If you received a qualifying distribution as a beneficiary after the participant's death, the participant must have been born before January 2, 1936, for you to use Form 4972 for that distribution.

Distributions to alternate payees. If you are the spouse or former spouse of a plan participant who was born before January 2, 1936, and you received a qualified lump-sum distribution as an alternate payee under a qualified domestic relations order, you can use Form 4972 to make the 20% capital gain election and use the ten year tax option to figure your tax on the distribution.

Consider this: A beneficiary of a taxpayer who is eligible for this option is also eligible to use the election. If the money is in the company plan and the retiree dies, the beneficiary retains this option to withdraw the funds in one tax year and use ten year forward averaging.

This option will not be favorable for all taxpayers, and must be calculated against other alternatives to determine which option appears best.

Communication point: If the taxpayer leaves one employer with assets that qualify for ten year averaging, he may keep that option if the assets are tallied into a conduit IRA, kept separate from other retirement funds, and later rolled into another employer's qualified plan.

Net Unrealized Appreciation (NUA)[1]

I own Company Stock in my Retirement Plan!

Many advisors driven to acquire IRA rollover accounts may fall short of reviewing or asking you if you had bought or own company stock in your retirement plan. Some people retire or leave a company, and in such cases, the tax law provides special optional tax benefits on that employer's stock. This stock is referred to as "Net Unrealized Appreciation" stock or "NUA shares" because these shares have hopefully been purchased at a lower price than their current value. Consequently, the share value contains unrealized appreciation.

Using the NUA strategy, individuals can take a distribution of employer's stock from their qualified plan and pay ordinary income tax only on their basis at the time of distribution (i.e. immediately), allowing for continued tax deferral on the balance of their shares. The difference between the basis and the fair market value at distribution—the net unrealized appreciation— is taxed at long-term capital gains rates when the stock is eventually sold, regardless of the holding period. Subsequent appreciation (earned after the distribution from the qualified plan) is taxed at short or long-term capital gains rates according to the length of the holding period, as measured from the date of the distribution continued tax deferral on the balance of their shares. The difference between the basis and the fair market value at

---

[1] Revenue Code (IRC) Section 402(e)4

IRA Misfortune 101

distribution—the net unrealized appreciation— is taxed at long-term capital gains rates when the stock is eventually sold, regardless of the holding period. Subsequent appreciation (earned after the distribution from the qualified plan) is taxed at short or long-term capital gains rates, according to the length of the holding period, as measured from the date of the distribution.

At first, it may seem crazy to pay tax immediately on any part of your distribution when you can do a rollover and defer all taxes. However, the following has made this a lower-cost strategy in some instances because of:

- The large spread between the max capital gains rate (15%) and the top ordinary income tax rate (35%).

- Large amounts of stock appreciation that oc-curred between 1982 and 2000.

Let's take a look at a simplified example, assuming tax rates of 15% for capital gains and 30% for ordinary income, and that your shares do not have additional appreciation after you leave your employer.

Over the years, you opted to have some of your 401(k) contributions invested in shares of your employer's stock. A total of $10,000 was invested in your employer's stock. Those shares are now worth $100,000. Your option is to have the stock distributed to you when you leave the company and pay tax on the basis (the $10,000 invested). Alternately, you could roll over all of the shares into your IRA and pay tax later, possibly decades later.

Below you see the difference in your options:

- Take stock and pay ordinary tax now on $ 10,000 (30%) and on the appreciation later at capital gains rate (15%) = total tax of $16,500.

- Roll over the shares to your IRA and pay tax at ordinary rates (30%) later, $100,000 = total tax of $30,000.

You save almost half of the tax by using the net unrealized appreciation rules.

NOTE: You may opt to use NUA treatment for only some of your employer's shares and rollover the rest.

Communication Point:

Many companies hold employer's stock in "stock funds", the units of which are composed of shares of stock and cash. These also are eligible for special NUA tax treatment if the plan provides for an "in-kind" distribution of stock from the plan. Although this is a long shot, it's worth asking if the shares in a stock fund can be distributed separately.

To take advantage of the NUA option, you must elect a lump sum, in-kind distribution from the plan (a complete distribution of all plan assets in a single calendar year). A lump sum distribution is defined as "distribution or payment within one taxable year of the recipient of the balance to the credit of an employee, which becomes payable to the recipient on account of the employee's death, after the employee attains age 59 1/2, on account of the employee's separation from service, or after the employee has become disabled."[2] Last but not least, keep in mind the use of NUA options does not require that you use it for all employer's shares. You may have 20,000 shares of your employer's/ ex-employer's stock, and you can decide to rollover 5,000 shares

---

[2] Sec. 402(e)(4)(D)(i)

and avoid current taxation and pay tax on the other 5,000 shares per the NUA rules. To maximize such a division, you want to obtain the cost basis of various lots of their stock from your plan administrator and review them to determine which shares might benefit most from the special NUA tax treatment. For example, it might make sense to use the NUA strategy on shares with the lowest cost basis relative to fair market value at distribution (and thus the greatest amount of NUA), and roll over shares with a higher cost basis relative to the fair market value at distribution.

The reduced 15% tax rate on eligible dividends and capital gains, previously scheduled to expire in 2008, has been extended through 2010 as a result of the Tax Increase Prevention & Reconciliation Act President Bush signed in 2006 (P.L. 109-222).

In 2011 these reduced tax rates will "sunset" or revert to the rates in effect before 2003, which were generally 20%. President Obama's budget, announced on February 25, 2009, calls for the Capital Gains Tax to be reverted to the 20% rate before the Sunset date of 2011.

This beneficial taxation on employer securities and ten year averaging can be used in combination. In order to do this, none of the distribution may be rolled to an IRA—the entire distribution must be taxed. You can elect to have just the cost basis or the entire value of the NUA shares subject to ten-year averaging. If there has not been much appreciation in your shares, it could pay to have the entire value taxed now under favorable ten year averaging rates. You know those bean counters in school we avoided; they became tax professionals and are now your best friend.

If you are one of those 401(k) participants that are considering ROTH conversion, pay particular attention to the new notice

FDIC & SIPC Insurance

Today appears to be the most challenging of times, with the volatility of the stock market, U.S. national debt is over 11 trillion dollars, 17 trillion dollars in retirement accounts, investor fraud, corporate giants disappearing in the night and government intervention in the business world. Interesting enough that since 2000, there have been over 90 bank failures, 71 of those failed in 2008 through June 2009. See a complete chart of these bank failures in (appendix 2). The chart below (Table 1.1) shows a snap shot of the number of failures for each year. The next chart (Table 1.2) is for bank failures through June 2009. It appears that if you had your assets allocated correctly based on the FDIC rules, you lost no money. Billions of dollars were handed over to financial institutions and corporations like peanuts. As this book goes to the publisher, 45 banks have collapsed and the FDIC has taken them over.

Table 1.1 Total Bank Failures this decade per Year

Thru June 2009	45	**2004**	4
2008	26	**2003**	3
2007	3	**2002**	11
2006	0	**2001**	4
2005	0	**2000**	2

Will this failure not double by the end of 2009?
I say most likely!

Table 1.2 Bank Failures for 2009 (for complete listing see Appendix)

Bank Name	CERT #	Closing Date
Mirae Bank, Los Angeles, CA	57332	26-Jun-09
MetroPacific Bank, Irvine, CA	57893	26-Jun-09
Horizon Bank, Pine City, MN	9744	26-Jun-09
Neighborhood Community Bank, Newnan, GA	35285	26-Jun-09
Community Bank/ West Georgia, Villa Rica, GA	57436	26-Jun-09
First National Bank of Anthony, Anthony, KS	4614	19-Jun-09
Cooperative Bank, Wilmington, NC	27837	19-Jun-09
Southern Community Bank, Fayetteville, GA	35251	19-Jun-09
Bank of Lincolnwood, Lincolnwood, IL	17309	5-Jun-09
Citizens National Bank, Macomb, IL	5757	22-May-09
Strategic Capital Bank, Champaign, IL	35175	22-May-09
BankUnited, FSB, Coral Gables, FL	32247	21-May-09
Westsound Bank, Bremerton, WA	34843	8-May-09
America West Bank, Layton, UT	35461	1-May-09
Citizens Community Bank, Ridgewood, NJ	57563	1-May-09
Silverton Bank, N.A., Atlanta, GA	26535	1-May-09
First Bank of Idaho, Ketchum, ID	34396	24-Apr-09
First Bank of Beverly Hills, Calabasas, CA	32069	24-Apr-09
Michigan Heritage Bank, Farmington Hills, MI	34369	24-Apr-09
American Southern Bank, Kennesaw, GA	57943	24-Apr-09
Great Basin Bank of Nevada, Elko, NV	33824	17-Apr-09
American Sterling Bank, Sugar Creek, MO	8266	17-Apr-09
New Frontier Bank, Greeley, CO	34881	10-Apr-09

Bank Name	CERT #	Closing Date
Cape Fear Bank, Wilmington, NC	34639	10-Apr-09
Omni National Bank, Atlanta, GA	22238	27-Mar-09
TeamBank, National Association, Paola, KS	4754	20-Mar-09
Colorado National Bank,Colorado Springs, CO	18896	20-Mar-09
FirstCity Bank, Stockbridge, GA	18243	20-Mar-09
Freedom Bank of Georgia, Commerce, GA	57558	6-Mar-09
Security Savings Bank, Henderson, NV	34820	27-Feb-09
Heritage Community Bank, Glenwood, IL	20078	27-Feb-09
Silver Falls Bank, Silverton, OR	35399	20-Feb-09
Pinnacle Bank of Oregon, Beaverton, OR	57342	13-Feb-09
Corn Belt Bank and Trust Company, Pittsfield, IL	16500	13-Feb-09
Riverside Bank of the Gulf Coast, Cape Coral, FL	34563	13-Feb-09
Sherman County Bank, Loup City, NE	5431	13-Feb-09
County Bank, Merced, CA	22574	6-Feb-09
Alliance Bank, Culver City, CA	23124	6-Feb-09
FirstBank Financial Services, McDonough, GA	57017	6-Feb-09
Ocala National Bank, Ocala, FL	26538	30-Jan-09
Suburban Federal Savings Bank, Crofton, MD	30763	30-Jan-09
MagnetBank, Salt Lake City, UT	58001	30-Jan-09
1st Centennial Bank, Redlands, CA	33025	23-Jan-09
Bank of Clark County, Vancouver, WA	34959	16-Jan-09
National Bank of Commerce, Berkeley, IL	19733	16-Jan-09

All dates are as of 6/30/2009 listed with FDIC website

IRA Misfortune 101

Seems like at least once a week, I am asked about these different insurance plans that protect their assets. So let's review these coverage's as it relates to the exposure of IRA account protection.

Let's first start by saying what should not need to be said, but I am going to say it anyway! IRA investments that buy stocks, mutual funds, real estate, land, bonds, are not covered for loss with FDIC or SIPC. However the SIPC members, which include most of the securities broker dealers, contribute to a reserve fund. This fund will reimburse up to $500,000 per customer, including up to $100,000 in cash. This coverage is for a brokerage firm failure and what seems to get media attention lately is broker theft. It's important to check your IRA custodial agreement, as many accounts that are over $500,000 may be covered with non-SIPC insurance, so check the details.

Example:

Mickey D. has his IRA account at XDFF On Line Brokerage Firm. He has invested over $49,500 in IRA contributions. His account grew to as high as $312,000 back in 1998. Today the value of his stocks and mutual funds lost $200,000 from 1998 to present. He has all this money invested into stocks and mutual funds. Unfortunately his account is down, and he is unable to recover any of this loss from SIPC. Mickey may want to consider a ROTH IRA conversion!

IRA accounts with banks and savings account associations, are federally insured up to $250,000 per bank through Federal Deposit Insurance Corp (FDIC). As most of you know, that limit was at $100,000. Credit Unions are insured by the, National Credit Union Administration (NCUA) up to $250,000. This coverage applies to SEPs, (Simplified Employee Pension) Roth IRAs, Savings Incentive Match Plans called SIMPLE, Self-

Directed employer sponsored defined benefit contribution plans, 401(k), Solo(k) known also as SIMPLE and traditional IRAs.

The rules under FDIC and NCUA cover all of an individual's retirements at the same insured bank. These accounts are added together and insured up to the $250,000.

Communication point: *The raise in coverage to the $250,000 per depositor has an expiration date of December 31, 2013. In January, 2014 the insurance amount returns to the $100,000 per depositor for all accounts, except IRAs and other certain retirement accounts, which will remain at $250,000.*

All Too Common Example:

A very intelligent attorney was looking to ladder his CDs so one would come due every two months. His IRA owns 6 C.D. accounts. His checking account had $9,000. The interest rate varied from 2.96% to 4.17%, each Certificate of Deposit worth $100,000. He smiled as he looked at me with that real self-confident look that only attorneys can give, and thought he was rather clever. He said: "See Tim, I really don't need an advisor. My IRA accounts are all doing fine. I am not losing one single nickel, each of my IRA accounts is insured up to $100,000." I explained to Mr. Doityourselfer he can have 100 accounts if he wants and have those CDs re- new every two weeks. The FDIC insurance only covers IRA accounts up to $250,000 per bank. If the bank fails, Mr. Doityourselfer will __suffer defeat__ in the amount of __$350,000.__ When the smoke clears, the federal regulators will tell him that $250,000 of the IRA account assets are all right and the additional $9,000 in his checking ac- count is all right as well, but the result is that the __$350,000 is lost forever__.

IRA Misfortune 101

Communication Point: *Hire an experienced set of eyes that specialize in IRA planning to help you maximize your own efforts, so you don't fall short in this area or possibly an area you have not reviewed because of education short sidedness*

Common Misperceptions about FDIC

- **The most a consumer can have insured is $250,000.**
  Wrong! Your accounts at different FDIC-insurance institutions are separately insured, not added together, when calculating the $250,000 limit. You might well qualify for more than $250,000 in coverage at each insured bank if you own deposit accounts in different "ownership categories." These categories include checking and savings accounts, retirement accounts, joint accounts and revocable trust accounts.

- **Changing the order of names or SSNs on joint accounts can increase the $100,000 coverage.** Not so! Rearranging the names listed on joint accounts, changing the order of Social Security numbers or renaming accounts from "Mary and John Doe" to "Mary or John Doe" will have no impact on joint account coverage. The FDIC adds each person's share of all the joint accounts at the same institution and insures the total up to $250,000.

- **Deposits in different branches of the same bank are separately insured.**
  Not true! FDIC insurance is based on how much money is in various ownership categories (single, joint, retirement, etc.) at the same insured institution. It doesn't matter if the accounts were opened at different branches, because they are all part of the same bank.

- **Any product sold by a bank is insured by the FDIC.**
  False! The FDIC insures deposits, such as checking accounts and certificates of deposit. It does not insure financial products such as stocks, bonds, mutual funds,

annuities or other insurance products, even when sold by a bank. FDIC-insured institutions that offer an investment product to a customer *are* required to disclose that the product is not FDIC-insured and is subject to investment

- **If a bank fails, the FDIC has up to 99 years to pay depositors for their insured accounts.**
  Complete nonsense! Scam artists trying to sell "financial" products sometimes use this myth to convince bank customers that they are wasting their time to place trust in FDIC-insured products. In fact, federal law requires the FDIC to pay the insurance deposits as soon as possible after an insured bank fails. We all have witnessed this over the past few years, via the news media or Internet.

- **My wife and I have multiple accounts in one bank, see our detailed list below: Are we FDIC covered and for how much?**

  A. Husband's single accounts have: $285,000 [$250,000]

  B. Wife's single accounts have: $210,000 [$210,000]

  C. Husband & Wife's Joint accounts have: 450,000 [$450,000]

  D. Husband's revocable trust accounts, wife as beneficiary, will have $1,000,000 [up to $250,000]
     $250,000 x 1 owner x 1 beneficiary.

  E. Wife's revocable trust accounts, husband and two children are beneficiaries. $250,000 [up to $750,000] $250,000 x 1 owner x 3 beneficiaries.

  F. Total cash in this bank is $2,195,000, Two accounts are over limits (a & d), One account is quite lower (e). The

IRA Misfortune 101

[ ] brackets represent the FDIC coverage for these accounts. Right now the maximum coverage for all of these deposit accounts are $1,410,000. Some rebalancing may need to occur with these accounts.

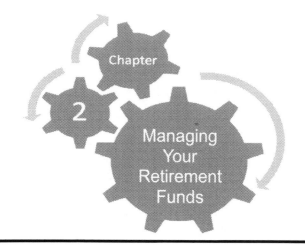

Chapter

2

Managing
Your
Retirement
Funds

Selecting a Custodian

IRA rollovers are ubiquitous, offered by every securities firm and many banks. You can basically buy many different products with your own IRA, then what does it matter which custodian you select?

Every custodian has an "adoption agreement" that contains restrictions that people and their advisors never read. A simple restriction may be that only publicly traded securities are permitted (stocks, bonds, mutual funds) but not privately traded securities, real estate, land, commercial properties. Other less obvious restrictions may be charges for transferring the account later or restrictions on your ability to set up your beneficiaries as you desire.

In fact, there are a number of boundaries. You and/or your advisor should read the adoption agreement that your custodian provides before opening the account. (Note—any IRA-savvy advisor will have already done this and selected their "favorite" custodians that offer the flexibility you desire). Don't be surprised if you ask your current advisor if he or she has read the custodian agreement and they say "Oh, that's all boilerplate—no one reads it." Get up out of your chair and run—fast. If you want to buy real estate and the custodian agreement does not allow your IRA to buy real estate through them, this may be a conflict with your goals.

Must Ask Custodian Questions:

IRA's have an IRA adoption agreement you will sign. Below are just a few questions you or your advisor should have answers to with regard to fashioning of your retirement plan goals.

- What are the annual fees and fees if you desire to transfer your IRA to another custodian?
- Will the custodian or plan administrator require that a designation of a beneficiary (s) be completed on their own forms? Will they accept it, as valid detailed, customized beneficiary designation created in conjunction with your retirement plan advisor?
- When death occurs, will the custodian permit your beneficiary or beneficiaries to receive payments over the period permitted by tax law and IRS rules and regulations, or will they mandate a shorter payout period?
- In the event of death, will the custodian permit your beneficiary or beneficiaries the amount of time granted by the tax law or IRS rules and regulations to choose among any available options, or will the custodian require a choice be made in a lesser time?
- Can I use my IRA money to purchase real estate, land or commercial property?
- Can I loan my IRA money to others and charge 10% cost of money rate to them?

- If I should die before my spouse, will the custodian permit my spouse or any of my beneficiaries to do a trustee-to-trustee transfer of the IRA account to a different custodian? At what fee?

- After my death, will the custodian permit the beneficiary of any portion of the account to name a subsequent beneficiary?

- Are my beneficiaries permitted (by their election or other wise) to take distributions over a term certain number of years? Will the custodian permit distributions over that period even if a beneficiary should subsequently die?

> **Also available, some additional questions to ask your custodian located in the Appendix of this publi-**

- Are one of those people that left your money at your former employer's 401(k) or profit sharing? Like custodians, the plan may have its own boundaries your beneficiary has with flexibility and tax planning techniques. In fact, my experience of 25 plus years continues to see many employer plans that have several restrictions on non-spouse beneficiaries. I know, unreasonable right! Kind of makes you wonder if part of the issue has to do with removing that person from the company plan to reduce plan participation cost to employer.

> **DOES YOUR ADVISOR DIRECT TIME AND ATTENTION TO BENEFICIARY (s) ?**

Ask yourself this: can you locate your copy of those beneficiary forms for every retirement account you own? Does the form have an official or stamped approval from the financial institution?

IRA Misfortune 101

Many clients I have counseled with expect the custodian or administrator to have these documents on file. What if the financial institution misplaces your beneficiary form, or improperly records your request? Mergers and acquisitions may cause a beneficiary form to get lost or even destroyed in the consolidation process. You may never know about it, _but your beneficiary (s) sure will, sorry to say, it may be too late._

After all, do you want your family to have a situation where the IRA custodian claims that you never provided a beneficiary form, especially since this would most likely become an issue when you are no longer around to dispute it? We will discuss more on this subject in the beneficiary selection, for now obtain a copy for each account you own!

Selecting Investments

Allowable Investments

In most cases, people will roll the funds over into their own IRA because this gives them better choices for investing. While 401(k), 403b, and 457 plans typically have limited investment choices, your own IRA permits you to make any investment permitted by IRS.[3]:

- Any publicly or privately traded security
- Real Estate (details later)
- Notes
- Annuities
- Vacation properties
- Hard money loans
- Tax Liens

---

[3] IRA Publication 590, 2009

- One, one-half, one-quarter, or one-tenth ounce U.S. gold coins, or one-ounce silver coins minted by the Treasury Department. It can also invest in certain platinum coins and certain gold, silver, palladium, and platinum bullion, but your IRA can not buy these other assets:

- Art works

- Rugs

- Antiques

- Metals

- Gems

- Stamps

- Life Insurance

- Alcoholic beverages

- Certain other tangible personal property.

Prohibited Transactions

Generally, a prohibited transaction is any improper use of your traditional IRA account or annuity by you, your beneficiary, or any disqualified person.

Disqualified persons include your fiduciary and members of your family (spouse, ancestor, lineal descendant, and any spouse of a lineal descendant). The following are examples of prohibited transactions with a traditional IRA.

- Borrowing money from it.

- Using the IRA as security for a loan.

- Selling your property to it.

- Receiving unreasonable compensation for managing.

- Buying property for personal use with IRA funds.

Fiduciary:

For these purposes, a fiduciary includes anyone who does any of the following:

- Exercises any discretionary authority or discretionary control in managing your IRA, or exercises any authority or control in managing or disposing of its assets.
- Provides investment advice to your IRA for a fee, or has any authority or responsibility to do so.
- Has any discretionary authority or discretionary responsibility in administering your IRA.

Effect on an IRA account—Generally, if you or your beneficiary engages in a prohibited transaction in connection with your traditional IRA account at any time during the year, the account stops being an IRA as of the first day of that year.

Significance to you or your beneficiary—If your account stops being an IRA because you or your beneficiary engaged in a prohibited transaction, the account is treated as distributing all of its assets to you at their fair market values on the first day of the year. If the total of those values is more than your basis in the IRA, you will have a taxable gain that is includible in your income. The distribution may be subject to additional taxes or penalties.

Borrowing on an annuity contract—If you borrow money against your traditional IRA annuity contract, you must include in your gross income the fair market value of the annuity contract as of the first day of your tax year. You may have to pay the 10% additional tax on early distributions, discussed in Chapter 3.

Pledging an account as security—If you use a part of your traditional IRA account as security for a loan, that part is treated as a distribution and is included in your gross income. You may have to pay the 10% additional tax on early distributions, discussed later.

Trust account set up by an employer or an employee association—Your account or annuity does not lose its IRA treatment if your employer or the employee association with whom you have your traditional IRA engages in a prohibited transaction.

Owner participation—If you participate in the prohibited transaction with your employer or the association, your account is no longer treated as an IRA.

Taxes on prohibited transactions—If someone other than the owner or beneficiary of a traditional IRA engages in a prohibited transaction, that person may be liable for certain taxes. In general, there is a 15% tax on the amount of the prohibited transaction and a 100% of the account is taxable if the transaction is not corrected.

Loss of IRA Status—If the traditional IRA ceases to be an IRA because of a prohibited transaction by you or your beneficiary, you or your beneficiary are not liable for these excise taxes, but the distribution may create some tax issues. However, you or your beneficiary may have to pay other taxes.

Real Estate in an IRA

Since this issue always seems to come up, let's address the possibility of using real estate as an IRA investment. Investment sales personnel can and will sell you a Real Estate Fund, Real Estate Investment Trust (can be public or privately traded) or a limited partnership. These are "paper" investments that typically do not give rise to the education you must arrange for yourself to properly own alternative investments like real estate, land, vacation homes, commercial properties, etc. The IRS does allow these type of investments for your IRA to buy. You can also use financing with purchases. I must say again, the education is a must, especially understanding cash vs. financing as it relates to Unrelated Business Income Tax issues (UBIT).

Visit our website: **www.IRARippleEffect.com**

How to Purchase Property with an IRA

Since every IRA must be held by an IRA custodian, you must first find a custodian that will permit this type of investment. Most banks and securities firm custodians will not permit it. Usually, a financial advisor can help you locate an independent IRA custodian that allows real estate investments and work with that company to set up an IRA account.

Section 408 of the Internal Revenue Code permits individuals to purchase land, commercial property, condominiums, residential property, trust deeds, or real estate contracts with funds held in many common forms of IRA's, including a traditional IRA, Roth IRA, Simplified Employee Pension plan, Solo (k) or SEP-IRA.

Purchasing the Property

Most IRA custodians that hold real estate will usually allow you to purchase raw or vacant land, residential properties, or commercial buildings for your portfolio. In addition, some custodians may permit foreign property or leveraged property.

Since buying a property may require more funds than you currently have available in your IRA, you also can have your IRA purchase an interest in the property in conjunction with other individuals, such as a brother, business associate or friend. Also keep in mind that if the property is leveraged, the debt must be a non-recourse promissory note.

Unfortunately, Internal Revenue Service regulations will not let you use the real estate owned by your IRA as your residence or vacation home. Nor can your business lease space in your IRA held property. The underlying premise for any real estate investment purchased with IRA funds is that you can't have any personal use or benefit of the property. To do so may cost you plenty in taxes and penalties.

There are a few other IRS limitations as well. You cannot place a real estate property that you already own into your IRA. Your spouse, your parents, or your children also couldn't have owned the property before it was purchased by your IRA. Property owned by siblings may be allowed, since the Internal Revenue Code (section 4975) specifies that only "lineal descendents" be disqualified.

Once you've chosen a property, your IRA custodian—not you personally—must actually purchase it. The title will reflect the name of your IRA custodian for your benefit (such as County Line Trust Company, Custodian FBO John Doe IRA). In addition, I recommend avoiding using personal funds for the initial transaction, this could make your deal a prohibited transaction.

Operating an IRA Property

Because all property expenses, including taxes, insurance, and repairs, must be paid from funds in your IRA, you'll need liquid funds available in your account. Of course, all income generated from the property will be deposited in your IRA account so you can use that money to cover your costs. But be very careful. If a storm blows the roof off the property and you need an instant $20,000, you can not write out a check. The money must come from the IRA, so you must always have significant liquidity in an IRA that holds real property.

It's also possible to sell properties while they are held by your IRA, so long as the purchaser is not a family member. Once a deal closes, your IRA account now holds the cash proceeds ready for you to make your next investment. An alternative is to sell an IRA-held property with seller financing so that all payments made by the buyers are paid to the IRA.

Communication Point:

You can deduct property taxes, mortgage interest, and you can use your depreciation deduction against income from that property in calculating UBTI (unrelated business taxable income). Also, if you used debt to finance the deal, selling the property could turn profit into ordinary income after allowable deductions and credits rather than capital gains that you would incur if your IRA owned the property with all cash.

Lifetime Tax Minimization

While everything in an IRA or qualified retirement plan grows tax deferred, it makes sense to own certain investments outside of an IRA in order to maximize the lifetime tax benefit. For example, if you hold shares of IBM for 20 years, the dividends are currently taxed at a maximum of 15% and current capital gains rates are 15%.

If those shares were owned in an IRA, the potential tax on the dividends and gains is 35%. When you hold the right investments in or out of a retirement plan, the savings can be several thousand dollars annually, which could compound to several hundred thousand dollars over a lifetime.

Communication Point:

Engage an expert advisor on these alternative IRA investments. If you ask your existing advisor about prohibited transactions or UBIT and he looks at you kind of funny, do not proceed forward. You are not the one to teach him/her how to help you! The education you can get will be worth the education cost and could be very profitable.

The next few pages will provide you with some very basic tax features on other types of investments.

Growth Mutual Funds

According to Morningstar[i], the average domestic stock mutual fund had a turnover rate of 97.5% This implies that the average stock in the fund was held about one year and a gain on the sale of stock held less than one year would be treated as a

---

[i]Morningstar Principia Pro 6/30/2005, average turnover of 10,444 funds categorized as "domestic stock" funds, data available upon request.

short-term capital gain. These gains would be passed along to the shareholder at a potential federal tax rate of up to 35%. In other words, high turnover is bad from the standpoint of taxes.

Therefore, growth mutual funds held outside of retirement accounts that generate much of their income as short term gains and taxed at rates up to 35% are taxed no worse than if held in an IRA and eventually distributed as ordinary income and taxed at 35%. When this fund is in an IRA, the gains do grow tax deferred. In this example it's best to hold growth funds inside an IRA because there are more beneficially taxed investments to hold outside of the IRA.

Short-Hold Stocks

Similar to the high turnover in mutual funds, gains on stocks bought and sold within one year are taxed at up to 35%. Therefore, if you plan to hold a stock less than one year, it is best purchased in a retirement plan, assuming you intend to make profit (losses unfortunately create no tax benefit when incurred within a retirement account). This will defer a gain that would be taxed at ordinary rates if achieved outside of your retirement.

Taxable Bonds/Bond Funds

Taxable bonds or bond funds from which the interest is not being used or distributed are best held inside a retirement plan.

Index or Low Turnover Funds

Index funds typically have low turnover. Therefore, gains are typically long term and taxed at rates up to 15%, as are the dividends. Index and low turnover funds are best held outside a retirement account. If held inside a retirement account, all distributions will be taxed as ordinary income at rates up to 35%.

Long-Hold Stocks

Hold outside of retirement accounts to enjoy long-term capital gain treatment and the preferable tax rate on qualified dividends.

Tax Free Bonds

Never hold these bonds in a retirement account. Doing so will convert tax free income into income taxable at a rate up to 35%.

Annuities

There's a big debate if annuities should be used inside an IRA or qualified plan. Typically, accountants focused only on tax issues, will argue that it makes no sense to have an annuity, whose primary benefit is tax deferral, inside a tax-deferred retirement account. But there's more to annuities than tax deferral.

Many annuities provide guarantees such as death benefits, guaranteed income benefits, or minimum return guarantees. Therefore, it could make sense to use annuities in retirement plans if you value these guarantees. Like any investment or insurance product, the issue is to compare the costs to the benefits. The same benefit may have a high value to you and a low value to another person, so there is no "right" answer about the best investment choices.

Concentrated Stock Positions

No matter how much you may love the company you retire from, do not keep a concentrated position of their stock, or any stock, inside or outside of your IRA. The risk in any one stock is just too great. Remember the companies that were investment darlings: Enron, WorldCom, Global Crossing, Conseco, Lucent, Qwest, Cisco, Sun Microsystems, Oracle. Investors who maintained concentrated positions in these stocks also concentrated their losses. The beauty of a concentrated position in an IRA is that you can sell it and diversify with no tax implications. Do it, and do it today.

Here's the research conclusion of a major investment research firm based on their 20-year study of concentrated positions:[5]

- *A single stock presents investors with an inferior risk/ reward profile.*

- *The higher volatility of an individual stock diminishes its expected long-term growth.*

- *Over the last 20 years, stocks with average volatility have lagged S&P level returns by nearly three percentage points per year. For the most volatile quartile of stock, the drag on performance has been close to seven points.*

- ***There is a pronounced skew to single-stock returns.** While the additional return potential for holding the right stock is substantial, significant underperformance has been four times as likely.*

- ***Reducing concentrated positions can help most investors achieve their long-term goals.** A minimum investment amount, tailored to the investor's circumstances, should be considered to ensure meeting spending needs. An optimal sale amount can be quantified, based on the investor's time horizon and risk tolerance, the tax cost of selling, the volatility of the single stock, and the level of portfolio concentration.*

---

[5] Bernstein Wealth Management Research, April 2004, "The Enviable Dilemma, Concentrated Stock" 2004 https://www. bernstein.com/ CmsObjectPC/pdfs/pub_ssb_0404_mod.pdf. Bernstein (previously Sanford Bernstein) is a wealth management division of Alliance Capital LP managing over $50 billion of assets.

If this warning is not sufficient for you, and you are convinced that you have a concentrated position in the greatest stock in the world, then at least hedge your bet. There are a few options other than selling:

Purchase a Put Option—A hedging strategy in which the investor wants to protect the downside price risk below the put price. The investor pays a premium upfront for downside protection below the strike price and is able to fully participate in the appreciation of the stock, minus the premium paid.

Zero-Premium Collar—A hedging strategy in which the investor simultaneously writes a covered call option and purchases a put option with equal premiums for a net zero out of pocket cost. The investor eliminates downside risk below the put strike price participates in the appreciation up to the call strike price and has full exposure to the stock volatility between the call and put strike prices.

The concentration of the position and appropriate action should be viewed in light of your entire net worth as part of your total financial planning. These options may not be available in your retirement account.

Moving Your IRA

When you rollover your IRA, you:

- Withdraw cash (or other assets such as stock, or mutual funds) from one qualified retirement plan or IRA account, then;

- Reinvest it (roll it over) in another qualified retirement plan or IRA account within a certain time limit (usually 60 days).

IRA Misfortune 101

Rollovers usually occur when you leave your job and receive all the funds in your retirement plan account. The most common rollovers are the movement of money:

- From one IRA to another IRA of the same type (traditional IRA to traditional IRA, or Roth IRA to Roth IRA).

- From an employer's plan to a traditional IRA.

- From one employer's plan to another employer's plan.

- From an IRA to an employer's plan.

If you have your plan administrator transfer the money from your qualified retirement plan account directly to an IRA account or another qualified retirement plan, that is a *direct rollover,* often called a trustee-to-trustee transfer, and is the preferable way to move money between retirement accounts as you will see.

Tax Reporting of Rollovers

From IRA to IRA

Here you transfer funds from a traditional IRA to another traditional IRA, or from a Roth IRA to another Roth IRA. The way you make the transfer dictates how much work you will face when you do your taxes.

When you ask your bank or other IRA custodian to do a direct transfer from your IRA account to another IRA account, the IRS does not require your bank to issue a Form 1099-R, which means that you do not have to report this transaction on your tax return.

.

If you pull money out of one IRA account yourself, then redeposit the money into another IRA account within 60 days, you need to report the rollover to the IRS, even though you do not have to pay any taxes on it.

The bank or custodian of the first IRA account issues you a Form 1099-R with the amount of the distribution shown in Box 1. As long as you actually redeposit the entire amount into another IRA within the 60-day time limit, you pay no tax on this rollover.

You report the amount from Form 1099-R box 1 on line 15a of Form 1040, and then enter a zero on line 15b (the taxable amount). (Note that these line numbers may change in the future).

In the margin next to line 15, you write the word _Rollover_ to signal to the IRS that these funds were in fact subject to a tax-free rollover. Keep documents proving that you deposited the money in another IRA within 60 days. You do not have to attach proof of the rollover to your return, but you should keep the documents in your records, in case the IRS has any questions about the rollover.

From Employer Retirement Plan to a Traditional IRA

If you ask your employer to transfer your retirement plan account balance directly to an IRA account when you leave your job, your employer's plan administrator will issue a Form 1099-R to you with the amount of the distribution in Box 1, and a letter code _G_ in Box 7. This indicates to the IRS that you rolled the money in your retirement plan over to an IRA account. This rollover is not taxed, however, you still need to report it on your tax return. Many people report the amount next to line 16, write the word "Rollover". The distribution code that is in Box 7 informs the IRS, Code G-is a direct rollover.

IRA Misfortune 101

For Example:

Distribution Code 1-Early Distribution, no known exception, (probably should write rollover on the 1040). Code 4-Death, if your seeing this one from your IRA, this is not good. Code B-Designated Roth Account distribution

With a direct rollover, no tax is withheld from any part of the distribution that is paid *directly* to the trustee of the IRA (or other retirement plan).

If you receive a distribution from your employer's plan, your employer or plan administrator will withhold federal income taxes at a 20 percent rate *even if you* deposit (or intend to deposit) the entire amount of the distribution (not just the amount you received a check for, but an amount equal to the gross distribution amount before withholding) in the traditional IRA or other plan within the 60-day period. Your employer's plan administrator will issue you a Form 1099-R, but the distribution code will be probably be 1.

> **Beware of Involuntary Taxation:** *If any part of that distribution is paid to you, that part is subject to 20 % federal income tax withholding and you wind up with a check containing 80 % of your retirement money. If you deposit (rollover) that 80 %, guess what: you owe taxes on the other 20 %, as if you had pocketed it yourself. You may even owe the 10% early withdrawal penalty tax. This is why it's best to NEVER touch retirement fund when you retire but have one custodian transfer the money to the other.*

Example

> *You have $10,000 in your employer's retirement plan, and your job is terminated. You request that the plan administrator issue you a check for the balance in your account. The plan administrator, however, must withhold 20 % of your distribution as federal income taxes, so you receive a check for only $8,000. The other $2,000 is sent to the federal government just like your payroll withholding.*

After the job loss shock wears off you open an IRA account within 60 days and deposit your $8,000 check in that account, not even thinking about this other $2,000. Tax time rolls around and your accountant informs you that the $2,000 is taxable as ordinary income. Since this money comes on top of other income, it pushed you into the 28% tax bracket,. Hold your horses my friend, you are also under 59 1/2. so you will pay an additional 10% penalty ($200) for early withdrawal.

This makes that $2,000 distribution a voluntary tax today of $760.

The best thing would have been for this person to come up with another $2,000 on his own and deposit that amount into the IRA account within the 60-day period. This way, your entire $10,000 distribution is considered a tax-free rollover.

Are you thinking, "What happened to the $2,000?" Assuming no other tax problems, the IRS will store the $760 in the IRS treasure chest and return the $1,240 to you. Wonder if they will put you on the birthday card list.

Special Note: There is no withholding on distributions expected to be less than $200 for the year.

From One Employer's Retirement Plan to Another

If you have money in a qualified retirement plan, such as a 401(k) plan, a 403(b) annuity, or a governmental 457 plan, you can roll over the distribution to any other such plan, if it is willing to take rollovers. Note: these plans are not required to accept rollovers; each plan has to choose whether or not to accommodate them. So check before you try.

IRA Misfortune 101

Examples of qualified retirement plans:

401(k) plans, 403(b) annuities, and governmental 457 plans.

If you have an administrator transfer money from one qualified retirement plan directly to another retirement plan, the first plan's administrator will issue a Form 1099-R to you with the amount of the distribution in Box 1, and a letter Code G in Box 7. As with a transfer from a retirement plan to an IRA, you are required to report this rollover on your return.

1. Report the amount from Form 1099-R Box 1 on line 16a of Form 1040.
2. Enter a zero on line 16b (the taxable amount).
3. In the margin next to line 16, write the word "Rollover".

If you made the transfer yourself (in other words, you took the money out of the first employer's retirement plan, then walked across the street and gave it to the second employer's retirement plan, within 60 days), you must report that rollover in the same way. Just be sure to hold onto the paperwork that proves you did this within the 60 day grace period.

No New Employer as of the 60 days:

There is a third alternative if you're moving money from one employer's retirement plan to another employer's retirement plan, you can temporarily move the money to an IRA before moving it to another employer. You might do this if you don't find a new employer within the 60-day time limit.

If you inherited the account from a spouse, you may roll over most distributions from the inherited account to a qualified plan, 403(b) annuity, or a government 457 plan in which you participate.

From IRA to Qualified Retirement Plan

You can rollover distributions from an IRA to a qualified plan, 403(b) annuity, or government 457 plan. These plans are not required to accept rollovers; each plan has to choose whether or not to accept your rollover or transfer.

Are There Time Limits on Rollovers?

You must contribute rollover funds to the replacement plan (either an IRA or another employer's qualified retirement plan) by the 60th day after you receive the distribution from the first IRA or qualified plan. It is important that you meet this deadline.

If you miss the deadline:

- The distribution is taxable in the year you received the money (not at the end of the 60-day time limit), and

- Money you contribute to a replacement IRA after that 60-day deadline is treated the same as a new IRA contribution, which means that it is subject to that year's limit.

If you're moving any retirement funds other than IRA funds, do a direct trustee-to-trustee transfer. This way you avoid getting hit with federal income tax withholding of 20%. Of course, you may try and apply for a PLR (Private Letter Ruling) from the IRS. However, The Office of Management and Budget announced that effective February 1, 2006 (IR-2005-144), the IRS will have new user fees! For example, the old days of paying $95 for a 60 -day rollover private letter ruling letter could be as high as $3,000 today. The fees for income individual tax payers are income based bias. Once you engage counsel (attorney, account- ant) these costs could rise to $15,000 to $20,000. Are you think- ing what I am thinking! Is the IRS seeing these transactions driven from bad advice, not bad tax code? Did IRS chief coun- sel decide to capitalize on it?

Advanced Management Strategies

#1:   You cannot roll over an IRA account more than once every 12 months. However, if you look to your IRA accounts for liquidity (not recommended), there is a way to ease the "once every 12 months rule." You can, in fact, lend yourself your IRA money year round if you split it into pieces.

Let's assume you have $120,000 in an IRA. You could take the $120,000 IRA and split it into six $20,000 IRAs (using a trustee transfer as described above). You can take $20,000 from the first IRA. Within 60 days, you replenish that $20,000 by taking $20,000 from the second IRA and so on with the six IRAs. In this manner, you have extended the 60 day rule into the 360 day rule (6 IRAs x 60 days each) to give yourself almost a year round loan. I don't recommend this strategy, as it can be complicated to manage. In addition, let's not forget about one of those IRS principals, "substance over form". That would be exploiting the tax rules! The fact that if you fail to complete a rollover or make a withdrawal from any single IRA more than once per 12-month period the tax and penalties could be upsetting.

Either violation will trigger the tax on your IRA and potentially a 10% penalty if you are under age 59½. A wise person once said: *"Use your bank teller to deposit and withdraw money, it is not beneficial to rely on the bank teller for these rules."* Weekly, I hear many examples of bad advice, which leads me to make this statement: *"All advice relating to IRA issues or direction should be followed up with supporting evidence that verifies the advisors recommendation."*

#2: You must rollover the same property. For example, if you distribute $50,000 from an IRA and buy a stock, you cannot roll that stock back into an IRA within 60 days and claim a 60-day rollover. You must deposit the same property   distributed.

120-Day Exception for First-Time Home Buyers

If you are retiring, it's unlikely that you will use your retirement money to buy your first home. However, it's possible you want to use that money to help the kids.

Taxable distributions of up to $10,000 from your IRA's are not subject to the 10% additional tax (early-distribution penalty) if the IRA owner or a qualified family member is a first-time home buyer and, within 120 days of receipt, the IRA owner uses the amount to pay for qualifying acquisition or rebuilding costs for his or her own, or qualifying family member's principal residence. If the amount is not used because of a cancellation or delay in the purchase or construction of the residence, the amount may be rolled over to the IRA within 120 days instead of the usual 60 days.

If you live in an area of the country where $10,000 would make a difference in the ability to purchase a home, send an email immediately (flatax27@hotmail.com) and let me know the location. Maybe it's a good place to have my IRA buy some properties.

Waiver

You may be asking yourself, "What if due to circumstances beyond my control, I don't complete a rollover in 60 days? What if I get in an accident on day 59? Don't bet on it, but the IRS has waived the deadline for "good Samaritans" making a good faith effort. Lets not forget about those new PLR fees.

The Economic Growth and Tax Relief Reconciliation Act of 2001 permits relief in certain hardship situations. In Revenue Procedure 2003-16, the IRS provides guidance, effective for eligible rollover distributions received after 2001, for obtaining an extension of the 60-day period. The IRS can grant an extension when failure to waive the 60-day requirement would be against equity or good conscience, including situations where a casualty, disaster, or other event beyond an individual's reasonable control prevented a timely rollover. The application procedure for relief is to obtain an IRS private letter ruling (PLR).

An Early Application

On February 28, 2003, the IRS received a request for a waiver of the 60-day rollover requirement from a married couple who had hired an investment manager to manage their investments, including their IRA investments. Without their knowledge, the investment manager took several distributions of their IRA assets for his personal use. The couple became aware of these misappropriations, which resulted in taxable distributions to them, after the 60-day rollover periods had expired.

They applied for a waiver of the 60-day. Their application indicated that a rollover of the distributed IRA assets would not violate the 12-month rollover rule, as there were no distributions   rolled over within the previous year

The IRS agreed (PLR 200327064 April 9, 2003) and waived the 60-day requirement, allowing the couple 30 days to roll over the misappropriated amounts. If they met all other rollover requirements, no federal income tax or 10 % penalty tax would apply to the involuntary distributions.

Remember only a Private Letter Ruling recipient can rely on what the IRS decides. For the rest of us, PLRs provide insight to the IRS reasoning. In this case, it is good to know that there is a possibility of relief from a 60-day rollover requirement missed due to certain involuntary acts or hardships.

In order to be considered for the waiver, you must submit an application for a private letter ruling (PLR) to the IRS and pay the applicable fee, which in 2005 was $95. That same fee today could be a low $625 and a high $2,500. The procedure for applying for a PLR is explained in the IRS publication, Revenue Procedure 2005-4. Any IRA owner who believes that he/she may be a waiver candidate should seek guidance from a tax or legal professional before filing an application with the IRS.

Can I Do a Partial Rollover?

Yes. Rolling over only part of the money in your retirement plan is called a partial rollover.

IRA Misfortune 101

Example:

> *Let's say you were terminated from your job and you have your old company send you your $8,000 in retirement savings. You needed $5,000 of that to live on while you were searching for a new job. You did manage to get the remaining $3,000 rolled over into your new employer's retirement plan within the 60-day time limit.*

> *The $3,000 you were able to successfully move to another plan in this partial rollover remains a tax-free transfer of tax-deferred funds. This is your partial rollover amount.*

> *The $5,000 you did not roll over is taxable according to whatever rules govern the taxation of your retirement income. Basically this means that you'll have to report the $5,000 on your income tax return. In addition, there is that 10 % early distribution penalty on that $5,000 if you received the money before age 59½.*

Caution With SIMPLE IRA rollovers

Rollovers involving SIMPLE plans are generally the same as rollovers from regular IRAs as long as the rollover occurs within two years after a contribution was first made to the SIMPLE IRA. During this two-year period, distributions can be rolled over *only* to another SIMPLE IRA.

If the amount you take out of a SIMPLE plan is deposited into a traditional IRA account within this two-year period, the distribution is not a tax-free distribution and the deposit into the traditional IRA is not a rollover contribution. What does this mean? You are subject to tax on the distribution amount, and your *contribution* to the traditional IRA may be subject to limitations based on your adjusted gross income.

After the expiration of the two-year period, you can roll over or transfer distributions from a SIMPLE IRA to a traditional IRA tax-free, or convert the SIMPLE IRA to a Roth IRA. As with traditional IRA accounts, you cannot roll over SIMPLE IRAs more than once every 12 months

After-Tax Contributions

Most contributions are pre-tax. You can contribute right up to the plan's limit, deducting all that money from your income before you pay taxes. Pre-tax, or deductible contributions, can generally be rolled over, following the rules.

But with some plans and IRAs, you can also put in additional money. Now, because these contributions are not tax deductible, you pay taxes on the money, so it is often called after-tax money. Those contributions may or may not be rolled over, depending on complicated rules you must understand.

Generally, employee after-tax contributions may be rolled over into another qualified plan or into a traditional IRA, except:

- If the rollover is from one qualified plan into another qualified plan, the rollover is permitted only through a direct rollover.

- A qualified plan can only accept rollovers of after-tax contributions if that plan provides separate accounting for those contributions and the earnings that will accumulate on those contributions.

- After-tax contributions and nondeductible contributions to a regular IRA still can't be rolled over from the IRA to a qualified plan, 403(b) annuity or government 457 plan.

Roth Conversion

The idea of converting a traditional IRA to a Roth (a tax-free IRA) gain several advantages:

- Allow the IRA funds to grow ***tax-free***.

- The Roth can be tax free to you, your wife, children, grandchildren and so on. Hey, you could even leave it to me. ALL TAX FREE

- No required minimum distributions

- Paying the income tax today may result in a lower tax paid as the account balance grows. Consider this, what if you are in a 30% tax bracket today and congress decides to raise your tax bracket to 40% or maybe higher as the account balance grows, the possibility of paying a higher tax could rise over the next few years.

In many of the Roth Conversions reviewed, the advisor had failed to calculate the lost opportunity cost on the asset removed from their asset page to pay the tax due on the IRA to Roth conversion.

It has been said that the conversion is only beneficial if you can pay the tax with non-IRA funds. Don't be fooled by some slick TV or Radio guru, you must study all the factors that will be in play in your world. At a minimum, look at the evidence as it relates to current taxes and future tax estimates, inflation, opportunity cost.

The other potential benefits of conversion I explain below:

- Because there are no mandatory distributions from a Roth IRA for people over 70½ , owning a Roth vs. traditional IRA may result in lower taxable income:

  a. The lower taxable income could possibly mean lower tax or no tax on social security income (since the taxation of social security income is based on the amount of adjusted gross income).

  b. In the case of a couple, when one spouse dies, and if the household income remains unchanged, the survivor's income taxes may rise (because single individuals pay more than married individuals for the same amount of income). By having a Roth IRA which does not require minimum distributions, the impact of the potentially higher tax bracket for the survivor is reduced

- Because the ROTH IRA account is not eroded by mandatory distributions, a larger, tax-sheltered account can be passed on to heirs. However, this can be bad from the standpoint of estate taxes, as the hopefully growing account increases the size of the estate.

- Because the Roth conversion tax must be paid at the time of conversion, the estate is immediately reduced by the amount of the income tax. This may appear to be favorable for a taxpayer with a taxable estate.

- An additional strategy may be to continue contributions to a Roth IRA past age 70½. You must have earned income. Traditional IRA does not allow contributions after 70½.

But even you want those advantages and are now running down to your IRA custodian convinced that you want to do a conversion. Wait. You may not qualify.

IRA Misfortune 101

For a single or married person filing jointly, if your adjusted gross income exceeds $100,000, you cannot convert. I know this may not be logical—why can a single man earning $99,000 convert, but if he marries a woman earning $2,000, and their adjusted gross income is now $101,000, neither of them can convert? No one said that tax laws were logical, but I suggest you obey them.

If you are contemplating marriage and a Roth conversion, have that difficult conversation with your fiancée. It may go something like this "I'm sorry dear, we must put off the wedding date until I complete my Roth conversion." Before she slams the door on her way out, inform your lovely bride to be that you also have added her as the beneficiary and she too, will receive this money tax free.

Communication Point:

The required mandatory distribution from your traditional IRA is not counted in that $100,000. So if you have $99,000 income from investments and $20,000 income from the mandatory distribution from your IRA (because you are past age 70½), only the $99,000 is counted for the conversion test.

Additionally, you may be able to engineer your income below $100,000 for one year in order to convert by:

- Deferring income.
- Moving investments to non-taxable accounts.
- Contributing to a 401 (k), 403(b), Keogh or SEP if eligible.
- Selling capital assets with unrealized losses (stocks, real estate).
- Any other action that will reduce your adjusted gross income.

For purposes of the $100,000 test, the amount that you convert, although it is taxable income, is not counted.

You don't need to convert your traditional IRA all at once. To spread out your tax bill, you can do partial conversions each year. If you haven't already left your home to go do this conversion, you may be asking yourself this clever question, "When I convert my IRA, do I need to do it during the calendar year before I know what my adjusted gross income will be for the year?" or "What if I convert and it exceeds $100,000?"

Good news! You have until the filing date of your return plus extensions (as late as October 15), to re-characterize the Roth and reverse the transaction like it never happened. You file an amended return if you have already filed before you do the re-characterization and all is right with the world, at least with the IRS.

Conversion Advantage

Let's take this hypothetical example. You worked for a company for many years, you just had your 50th birthday and have built up your 401(k) account and upon retirement, rolled it to a traditional IRA. Now, you want to re-title the $300,000 traditional IRA to a Roth IRA.

Next you will see the difference over 20 years, assuming a hypothetical earning on the funds at 6% and a combined tax bracket of 33%.

When we do this comparison, we must account for the asset you show on your asset page if you <u>do not</u> convert to a Roth. You see that below as "Municipal Bond". It's the $99,000 you would have paid in tax on a Roth conversion (33% x $300,000), invested at 4.5 in the municipal bond that would grow to $238,760 after 20 years.

Table 2.1 Study the Evidence

Most advisors, including TV gurus and internet or YOU TUBE favorites, neglect to consider opportunity cost in their overall evaluation. Many advisors use similar tables below to convince you to make the conversion! They call these: apples-to-apples comparison and construct a case that makes you believe there is a $300,000 gain in this hypothetical situation using the Roth, keeping money at work growing tax-free for a long period.

	Roth IRA	*Traditional IRA*
Balance Today	$300,000	$300,000
Balance in 20 Years	$962,140	$962,140
Tax Due 20th Year	$0.00	-$317,506
Tax paid Today from other asset	**$99,000**	0.00
Value after tax is paid	$962,140	$644,634
Tax Free Growth & Distribution	YES	NO

Advisors micro view shows a $317,506 advantage completing the Roth Conversion, depleting a cash asset in the process. He fails to show the true cost of depleting the asset, (**lost opportunity cost**).

Table 2.2 Apply the Truth

When you use a cash asset or income to pay tax, you miss the opportunity that the cash asset or income will create for you over time.

	Roth IRA	*Traditional IRA*
Balance Today	$300,000	$300,000
Balance in 20 Years	$962,140	$962,140
Tax Due 20th Year	$0.00	-$317,506
Municipal Bond Value 20 Years	$0.00	+$238,760
Lost Opportunity Costs	-$238,760	0
Value after tax and Muni Bond	$723,380	$833,394
Tax Free Growth	YES	NO

Lost opportunity cost is the future value of the municipal bond value of $238,760, bringing your cost on the conversion to $160,014. in reduced wealth. You pay a lower tax bill on a conversion today, the deception is you actually have less wealth in the future.

How To Do A Roth Conversion

You have three choices:

1. You can do a rollover (within 60 days as we discussed before),

2. You can do a trustee to trustee transfer,

3. If you like your account just where it is, you can have the existing trustee "re-designate" the IRA to a Roth.

Even if you are under age 59 ½, the penalty does not apply when you move money from a traditional IRA for the purpose of converting.

IRA Misfortune 101

Case studies on other Roth conversions that also have incomplete information.

An Advisor Story:
Harry is 50 and single. He has a $1 million traditional IRA and other non-IRA assets valued at $1,000,000 that put his estate in the 55% marginal tax bracket after 2011. Even though in 2009 it's 45%, he has no estate tax that will be due if death occurs. In 2010 the estate tax is repealed, in 2011 the old estate tax exemptions are reverted and the estate tax exemption falls back to $1,000,000. Harry understands the Roth's benefits but is less than enthusiastic about paying $350,000 in income tax (35% federal, state not included) for the conversion.

He rationalized that he doesn't have enough years to make up the out-of-pocket tax cost. However, a review of the tax savings for his heirs convinced him differently, and he made the conversion.

Since Harry reduced his estate by $350,000 (income tax paid on the conversion), he cut his potential estate taxes by $192,500. Thus, the IRS picked up part of the cost. And his beneficiaries stand to inherit his $1 million Roth IRA from which they can withdraw income for the rest of their lives, income tax-free. Otherwise, if the funds had been left in the IRA, they may have had to pay up to 35% on the distributions.

The possible tax savings:

Estate Tax	$192, 500
Income Tax	$350,000
Total:	$542,500

TIM SAYS: Suppose that Harry lives another 15 or 20 (Table 2.3) years and earns 7% on his retirement funds. (Illustration does not reflect Harry's RMDs.)

Table 2.3:   Roth IRA Protection

	Traditional IRA	Roth IRA
15 Years	$2,759,032	$2,759,032
Income Tax to Heirs	$965,566	$0.00
20 Years	$3,869,684	$3,869,684
Income tax to Heirs	$1,354,389	$0.00
Proceeds (less Estate Taxes)	$2,515,295	$3,869.684

Did you notice, that in the advisor's story he failed to mention opportunity cost of the asset used to pay the tax and what that asset's performance (5%, 6%, 7%, 8%) value was? The cost at just an LOC rate of 7% could result in a 1.3 million expense. This cost must be presented to give this recommendation merit. In addition, the estate tax of 1.5 million was not accounted for in the "Income Tax to Heirs" category in year 15, and 2.2 million in year 20 "Income Tax to Heirs" projections. Please don't allow yourself to fall into this kind of deception.

Advisor Story #2

Bill has a $2 million IRA. The only other asset is a $500,000 home that he owns with his wife, Linda. Together, they have a 42-year-old son, Ted.

Bill should leave his IRA to Ted. Hence when Bill dies, Ted will receive the $2 million estate tax-free ($2 million exemption in 2006). Ted will then be able to stretch out the distributions over his lifetime, thereby adding decades of tax-deferred growth to the IRA.

Linda, however, also needs $1 million to support herself when Bill dies.

Bill takes a distribution from the IRA and uses money to buy a $1 million life insurance policy on his life and names Linda the beneficiary. There will be no estate taxes because _of the unlimited marital deduction. Furthermore, Linda will get the $1 million income tax free rather than a tax-riddled IRA._

When Bill dies, Ted will receive whatever is left in the IRA. Linda will have $1 million to spend as she wishes without worrying about taxes or RMD regulations.

However, suppose Bill likes the idea that a Roth IRA passes income tax free to beneficiaries, but he doesn't have the $700,000 to pay the tax on a conversion?

Bill could buy a $1 million life insurance policy and name Linda the beneficiary on the policy as well as on the IRA.

When Bill dies, Linda receives the life insurance proceeds and the IRA. She rolls the IRA into her IRA. As long as her income is not over $100,000, she can convert the $1 million rollover to a Roth IRA. She'll use $700,000 from the life insurance proceeds to pay the income tax..

Linda's Roth IRA will not be subjected to RMD, She'll never have to withdraw money, and any funds that she does take out are income tax free. When she dies, her heirs will receive the Roth income tax free. But, if her account grows so much that there could be an estate tax problem, Linda may be directed to use a trust to buy a life insurance policy to pay potential taxes. When considering an irrevocable trust, you must consider the additional opportunity cost to your estate.

Linda's beneficiaries will receive the death proceeds income and estate tax free, and use the funds to pay the estate tax on Linda's Roth.

What if You Cannot Convert Because Your Income is Too High?

You may exceed the $100,000 income threshold precluding conversion. This simply means that any IRA money you don't spend during your lifetime will be subject to income tax and potentially estate tax later. You can offset these taxes with life insurance as explained later.

> The year of 2010 will be an interesting year....thanks to The Tax Increase and Prevention Act (TIPRA). Beginning January 1, 2010 the income threshold of $100,000 is removed for IRA to Roth Conversions. Regardless of your income you will be qualified to do the conversion. This opens up the door for all taxpayers to convert IRA accounts to Roth IRAs.

> The IRS added a perk, you will have the option to spread the income tax due on the conversion over two years. A small communication point spreading the tax could trigger additional tax should congress increase tax rates. Should your asset value be lower prior to conversion, this could be a conversion advantage to you.

> In addition, based on current tax law 2010 if this is that last year on earth for you, there is no estate tax. No matter how much you have in assets, it will all flow estate tax free to your heirs. In 2011 the estate tax is scheduled to come back in at $1,000,000 exemption per person.
> Can you guess what Congress will do with this?

IRA Misfortune 101

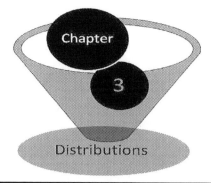

Distributions

Just the Facts....On June 4, 2009 I received a note from Senator George Voinovich, telling me that my share of the U.S. Debt is $36,683 and our U.S. debt is over 11.2 trillion dollars. These are the facts.....Let's play a game. Take your retirement plan account value and apply a tax bracket of 25%. Does this number represent your share of U.S. Debt? Is your deferred tax payment on this money considerably higher? Let's review an example. You have $180,000 in an IRA or 401(k). This computes to a $45,000 tax being deferred, tax rates climbing to 40% would be $72,000, a difference of $27,000. Maybe that is why the   current administration seems to not care about this compounding debt. Build it, they (being the IRS) will come. Compounding your hard earned money seems to benefit others. That was fun! Lets get started on distributions.

Mandatory Distributions

IRS imposes some stiff penalties if you miss your required minimum distributions. If you take advanced distributions before 59½, and the beneficiary does not take RMDs on an inherited IRA there can have additional costs from 10% to 50% of the distribution taken or to be taken. Think about it, many years ago it took you 18 seconds to write a check for a deposit into your retirement account.

YOU MUST NOW PLAY BY THE IRS RULEBOOK

IRA Misfortune 101

If you are the owner of a traditional IRA, you must start receiving distributions from your IRA by April 1 of the year following the year in which you reach age 70½. April 1 of the year following the year in which you reach age 70½ is referred to as the Required Beginning Date (or RBD). You must receive at least a minimum amount for each year starting with the year you reach age 70½ (your 70½ year). If you do not (or did not) receive that minimum amount in your 70½ year, then you must receive distributions for your 70½ year by April 1 of the next year.

As a practical matter, even though you have until April 1 of the year after you reach age 70 ½ to take your first distribution, waiting will require you to take two distributions that year (one by April 1 for the prior year and another distribution by December 31 for the current year). Taking two distributions could significantly raise your taxes and marginal tax bracket unnecessarily. It may trigger your social security income to become taxable or create additional tax on your social security income, and preclude you from maximizing your itemized deductions.

If an IRA owner dies after reaching age 70½ but before April 1 of the next year, no minimum distribution is required because death occurred before the required beginning date.

If you miss a distribution, you must pay a 50% penalty and still take the distribution.

The divisor you must use to figure the distribution amount each year is per the following table 3.1.

Table 3.1 Uniform Lifetime Table used for RMD Calculations

AGE	DISTRIBUTION PERIOD	AGE	DISTRIBUTION PERIOD
70	27.4	93	9.6
71	26.5	94	9.1
72	25.6	95	8.6
73	24.7	96	8.1
74	23.8	97	7.6
75	22.9	98	7.1
76	22.0	99	6.7
77	21.2	100	6.3
78	20.3	101	5.9
79	19.5	102	5.5
80	18.7	103	5.2
81	17.9	104	4.9
82	17.1	105	4.5
83	16.3	106	4.2
84	15.5	107	3.9
85	14.8	108	3.7
86	14.1	109	3.4
87	13.4	110	3.1
88	12.7	111	2.9
89	12.0	112	2.6
90	11.4	113	2.4
91	10.8	114	2.1
92	10.2	115 and over	1.9

NOTE: Do not use this table if IRA Owner has spousal beneficiary that is 10 years younger. See IRS Publication 590 and use Joint Life Table.

IRA Misfortune 101

Here's how you figure your required minimum distribution.

1. Take your IRA balance as of the previous December 31.

2. Divide by the number from the previous page, (Table 3.1) that matches the age you attain this year.

3. The result is the amount you must distribute from your IRA.

Generally, you pay tax on this amount unless part of your IRA is from non-deductible contributions.

Enforced Distributions - - Uniform Lifetime Table

For use by:

- Unmarried owners.

- Married owners whose spouses are not more than ten years younger.

- Married owners whose spouses are not the sole beneficiaries of their IRAs.

Example: Age: 70½	Example Age: 71
IRA balance $136,000	IRA Balance $139,200
Divisor 27.4	Divisor: 26.5
RMD $4,963.50	RMD: $5,252.83

For example, say that out of your $30,000 IRA contributions, $3,000 were non-deductible (e.g. 10% of your total contributions). When you make a distribution, 10% is counted as being the non-deductible contributions, so you pay tax on 90% of your distributions. Keep in mind that the taxable amount for your federal tax return may not be the same for your state tax return. That's because when you made contributions, your state may not have allowed you to fully deduct the contribution so some of your distributions will not be taxed for state purposes.

Generally, people like to take the minimum required amounts from their IRA each year because they want to defer the tax payment as long as possible. You may be pleased to know that you can use a more beneficial table (with smaller annual distributions amounts) if your spouse is your sole designated beneficiary and is more than ten years younger than you.

Account Aggregation

In order to determine your balance as of December 31 of the previous year, you aggregate accounts of the same type:

> IRAs, SEP-IRAs, SIMPLE IRAs get aggregated.

> *NOTE: Inherited IRAs do not get included here—they have their own category and only inherited IRAs from the same decedent can be aggregated. Additionally, if you have named a spouse as the sole beneficiary on any IRA, and the spouse is more than ten years younger, you must calculate the distribution on that account separately.*

You can aggregate together all 403(b) accounts as you do with IRAs.

Once you total the balance from the category and calculate the distribution, you are permitted to take the distribution from any one or all of the accounts in that category.

Qualified plans (Keogh, 401(k)) cannot be aggregated, and the minimum distribution must be calculated and distributed from each plan.

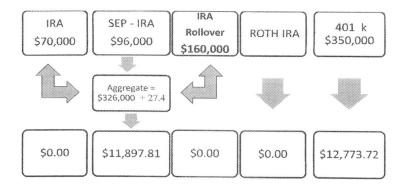

Taking Distributions Early

Based on what we just covered about wanting to defer distributions to defer taxes, why would anyone in their right mind take distributions early? It can actually save taxes in certain situations.

Example:

Bill and Linda are both retired, have large IRAs, and are 60 years old. Their taxable income will be $30,000 this year.

The new tax law extends the 15% tax bracket to $67,900 for couples filing jointly (see table below). Thus, Bill and Linda could distribute (or convert to a Roth) $37,900 worth of their IRAs to this year and fully use up their 15% tax bracket.

The federal income tax rate on the $37,900 distribution will be 15% ($5,6895). Some states require income tax on this distribution.

If Bill and Linda had waited until they were 70½ and subject to required mandatory distributions, those larger distributions may have pushed their income into a higher tax bracket. Therefore, sometimes it pays to pay tax early if you do so at a lower rate.

Table 3.2: — Married Filing Jointly 2009

If Taxpayer's Income is Over	But Not Over	The will be :
$0.00	$16,700	10%
$16,701	$67,900	15%
$67,901	$137,050	25%
$137,051	$208,850	28%
$208,851	$372,950	33%
$372,950	And over	35%

Roth Distributions[7]

We talked about Roth conversions earlier. Now let's look at how you get the money out of a Roth. You first want to do some careful planning here. These funds are really special as they grow tax-free. Some people get confused and think they should spend interest before they spend principal. So they will spend the earnings on their IRA before they spend their non-IRA principal. However, this does not minimize their tax situation.

Your non-IRA money has already been taxed, so it might as well be used first. Your IRA money is either tax deferred or tax free, in the case of a Roth, so you want to leave it untouched. In other words, from a tax standpoint, it's better to spend down your non-IRA principal before touching any of your ROTH IRA money. Since there is no difference between principal and interest (it's all green), you should forget the distinction because it's all your money and does not matter how you label it. The whole idea of principal and interest is something we made up. So you see why allowing your ROTH IRA money to grow is likely preferable. (Financial planners have software that can answer the question of which "buckets" of money should be used first for potential lifetime tax minimization). With 25 years of experience, this author has only found one company that can show scientific, verifiable evidence on the best distributions for you: Leap Systems, Inc.

Additionally, there may be restrictions for removing money from a Roth conversion. Here's how they work.

First, if you are younger than 59 ½ and you remove money from a Roth within five years of conversion, you will owe a 10% early withdrawal penalty. (Note that the five year measurement for Roth conversion distributions starts from the first day of the tax year in which the conversion is made.)

---

[7] IRS Publication 590 contains the Roth distribution rules summarized here

IRA Misfortune 101

Next, when you withdraw funds, IRA classifies each
dollar as follows in this order:

1. Roth contributions (assuming you did a conversion
    and it's the first time you have had a Roth, this will
    be zero).
2. Roth conversion money, in chronological order if
    more than one, first the taxable amounts and then any
    non-taxable amounts rolled over of each conversion.
3. Earnings on Roth contributions or conversions.
4. See Tables 3.3 and 3.4 on the following pages.

Allowed Exceptions for Roth Distributions if Under Age 59½ (see table 3.3, pg 65)

- A first-time home purchase (lifetime maximum is
  $10,000)
- Post-secondary education expenses
- Substantially equal periodic payments taken under IRS
  guidelines
- Medical expenses exceeding 7.5% of your adjusted gross
  income
- An IRS levy
- Disability
- Death
- Health insurance premiums
  (exception available after you have received at least 12
  consecutive weeks of unemployment compensation)

Table 3.3: Roth distributions if <u>under age 59½</u>:

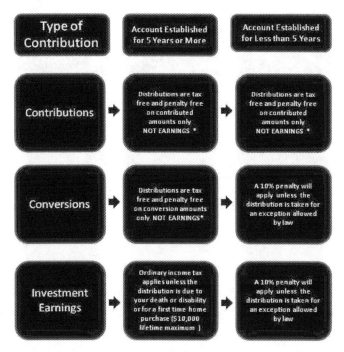

* Earnings on Contributions and Converted assets are subject to ordinary income taxation and 10% penalty if you are younger than 59½ years old. See Publication 590 and IRC Sec 408A(d)(2)(B)

Each Roth **_conversion_** starts a new five year clock until you have reached the age requirement of 59½. However, the five year clock for Contributions starts the year the first contribution is made and subsequent deposits are not subject to the five year rule.

Example: Joe made a contribution to his ROTH IRA on Dec 30, 2009 in the amount of $5,000. His five year clock started January 1, 2009. So in January 1, 2014 he would be able to withdrawal the $5,000 contribution made on December 30, 2009 without penalty. Effectively making this a 48 month hold period. Joe also made an additional deposits each year going forward. These additional contributions still revert to the January 1, 2009 date. He could than withdrawal all contributions regardless of contribution date because the five year rule relates to the January 1 tax year in which the account was originally set up.

Table 3.4: Roth distributions if <u>over age 59'/₂</u> :

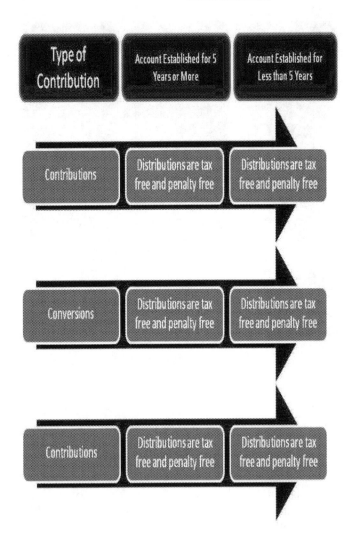

Type of Contribution	Account Established for 5 Years or More	Account Established for Less than 5 Years
Contributions	Distributions are tax free and penalty free	Distributions are tax free and penalty free
Conversions	Distributions are tax free and penalty free	Distributions are tax free and penalty free
Contributions	Distributions are tax free and penalty free	Distributions are tax free and penalty free

NOTE: On Conversions any individual who has reached the age of 59½ are immediately entitled to a tax free and penalty free distribution.

Let's assume you have no Roth contributions and that you are age 62. You only have converted amounts in your Roth. You are free to make distributions at any time, and you will pay tax on any earnings if the account is not five years old, as determined by the earliest conversion. After five years, all distributions are tax-free. Let's assume you have no Roth contributions and that you are age 62. You only have converted amounts in your Roth. You are free to make distributions at any time and you will pay tax on any earnings if the account is not five years old, as determined by the earliest conversion.

After five years, all distributions are tax-free. As a practical matter, prior to five years after conversion, very little of the money will be earnings— it will be mostly the converted balance. And since the converted balance is deemed by IRS to be withdrawn before earnings, you can withdraw most of your Roth balance without tax because the earnings amounts are considered withdrawn last.

Regarding mandatory distributions—there are no mandatory distributions for the owner of a Roth IRA or the spouse that inherits. But a non-spouse beneficiary must make mandatory distributions over his or her life expectancy. The penalty is 50% of the amount not taken.

Pre-59½ Distributions

You may be among those that retire early and want to use your retirement funds. The problem is, though, you will have to pay the 10% early withdrawal penalty. Fortunately, there is a way around this.

IRA Misfortune 101

Section 72(t) of the Internal Revenue Code allows taxpayers of any age to take a series of substantially equal periodic payments without a 10% penalty.

The payments must continue for five years or until you reach 59 ½ years old, whichever period is longer. While you receive the money, you cannot make any changes to the payments. However, you can irrevocably switch one time to the RMD method.

If you do not stay with the plan, or if you modify the payments in any way, you will no longer qualify for the exemption from the 10% penalty. Furthermore, the 10% penalty will be reinstated retroactively, to all prior years.

Each IRA stands on it own, meaning that taking 72(t) distributions from one account has no effect on the others. Therefore, if one IRA will produce more income than is needed, you could set up a smaller, segregated account to withdraw from. And in the future, if you need more income, you could begin equal distributions from another account as well. This could provide greater flexibility in meeting your immediate and future income requirements.

Activation of 72(t) Distributions

Lets review the three ways to calculate 72(t) distributions.

The **Minimum Distribution Method** is calculated the same way as required minimum distributions when account owners reach their required beginning distribution date. This method will generally produce the lowest annual 72(t) payments since it is based on the longest life expectancy. The required minimum distribution method consists of an account balance and a life expectancy (single life or uniform life or joint life and last survivor) each using the age (s) attained in the year for which distributions are calculated. The annual payment is re-determined for each year.

This is the simplest of methods to calculate and allows seniors to take advantage of growth in their accounts, and create larger payments in future years. However, a decline in the IRA balance will reduce future 72(t) distributions.

The *Fixed Amortization Method* consists of an account balance amortized over a specified number of years equal to life expectancy (single life or uniform life or joint life and last survivor), and a rate of interest that is not more than 120 percent of the federal mid-term rate published in revenue rulings by the service. Once an annual distribution amount is calculated under this fixed method, the same dollar amount must be distributed in subsequent years.

This produces higher payments than the Minimum Distribution Method and gives some security in that the payments are fixed. But the calculation is complicated, and there is the risk that the payments will not keep pace with inflation, or the account will not be able to sustain the payments if there is a significant downturn in the market.

The Fixed Annuitization Method

This consists of an account balance, an annuity factor, and an annual payment. The age annuity factor is calculated based on the mortality table and according to IRS Notice 89-25, the interest rate used must "not exceed a reasonable interest rate on the date payments are to commence." The service went on to define reasonable interest rate that is not more than 120% of the

IRA Misfortune 101

Once an annual distribution amount is calculated under this fixed method, the same dollar amount must be distributed under this method in subsequent years. **The federal mid-term rates can be found at the IRS web site:** http://www.irs.gov/businesses/small/article/ **0,,id=112482,00.html**

This method may at times provide the largest payments, depending on the size of the account and interest rates used. And like the amortization method, the payments are fixed.

Required Minimum Distribution Method Example:

The annual distribution amount ($11,695.91) is calculated by dividing the end of year account balance ($400,000) by the single life expectancy (34.2).

$$\$400,000/34.2 = \$11,695.91$$

For subsequent years, the annual distribution amount will be calculated by dividing the account balance as of December 31 of the prior year by the single life expectancy obtained from the same single life expectancy table using the age attained in the year for which distributions are calculated. For example, if Harold's IRA account balance, after the first distribution has been paid, is $408,304 on December 31, the annual distribution amount for next year ($ 12,261.38) is calculated by dividing the December 31 account balance ($408,304) by the single life expectancy (33.3) obtained when an age of 51 is used.

$$\$408,304/33.3 = \$12,261.38$$

Fixed Amortization Method Example:

For the first year, the annual distribution amount will be calculated by amortizing the account balance ($400,000) over a number of years equal to Harold's single life expectancy (34.2) when an age of 50 is used at a rate of interest equal to 2.8%. If an end-of-year payment is calculated, then the annual distribution amount is $18,328.00. Once an annual distribution amount is calculated under this fixed method, the same amount will be distributed under this method in subsequent years.

Fixed Annuitization Method Example:

Under this method, the annual distribution amount is equal to the account balance ($400,000) divided by the cost of an annuity factor that would provide one dollar per year over Harold's life, beginning at age 50 (i.e. the actuarial present value of an annuity of one dollar a year payable for the life of a 50 year old). The age 50 annuity factor (21.901) is calculated based on the mortality table from the IRS, per Revenue Ruling 2002-62 and an interest rate of 2.80%. Such calculations would normally be made by an actuary.

The annual distribution amount is calculated as

$$\$400,000/21.901 = \$18,264.00$$

Once an annual distribution amount is calculated under this fixed method, the same amount will be distributed under this method in subsequent years.

Case Example:

Heather has $1 million in her IRA, is 57, and wants to retire. She'll have enough to live on once Social Security starts at age 62. However, until that time, she will need an additional $12,000 per year to meet her living expenses.

IRA Misfortune 101

The IRA is her only investment asset. But she doesn't want to pay the 10% penalty on early withdrawals for the next 2 1/2 years. How much should Heather convert for Section 72(t) distributions?

The three distribution options would require that Heather commit the following amounts for Section 72(t) distributions:

> *Minimum Distribution Method—$334,800*

> *Fixed Amortization Method—$230,220*

> *Fixed Annuitization Method—$230,780*

Since Heather does not want to withdraw any more than necessary, segregating $230,220 and using the Fixed Amortization Method for Section 72(t) distributions is the most desirable strategy. This will give her $12,000 per year for five years until her Social Security begins.

Heather will also have the flexibility to take money from her remaining $769,780 IRA without paying the 10% penalty after she turns 59 1/2.

It is absolutely necessary to review your plan as it relates to Estate Taxes each year, for the next three years! With the Estate Tax Exemption this year at 3.5 million, going to an unlimited exemption in 2010 to 1.0 million in 2011. This is a rollercoaster ride that you must not remain seated.

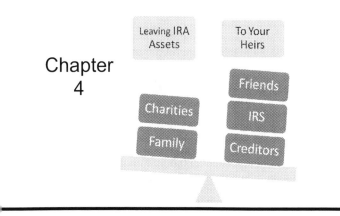

Chapter 4

Understanding Estate Taxes

Your IRA will be eroded by income taxes, inflation and quite possibly estate taxes. So we must take a quick look at how estate taxes work. Mind you, some think that the estate tax has been repealed or will be repealed. This is incorrect and within minutes, you'll know more than your friends on this issue and be able to dazzle them in the break room at work.

What is the Estate Tax?

The estate tax is a tax on accumulated wealth in excess of predetermined congressional guidelines. So when you die and you are considered wealthy (by the estate tax rules at your death), your estate is subject to this additional tax. During one of my recent seminars an attendee asked, "Is this the government's way of making sure no family gets 'too rich' by passing wealth from generation to generation?"

Your gross estate includes the value of all property in which you had an interest at the time of your death, including all retirement accounts. Your gross estate also will include the following:

- Life insurance proceeds payable to your estate or, if you owned the policy, and it was paid to your heirs.
- The value of certain annuities payable to your estate or to your heirs.

- The value of certain property you transferred within three years before your death.
- Trusts or other interests established by you or others in which you have certain powers.

Your taxable estate is your gross estate less the allowable deductions:

- Funeral expenses paid out of your estate,

- Debts you owed at the time of death, and

- The marital deduction (generally, the value of the property that passes from your estate to your surviving spouse).

You see that one of the allowable deductions from your estate is property that you leave to a spouse. But this is no gift from the IRS. Assets you leave to a spouse become part of the surviving spouse's estate and will be taxed when the surviving spouse dies.

Take a look at Figure 4.1. We have a hypothetical example of a couple with $3.5 million of assets. For 2009, each person can pass $3.5 million estate tax free. As a reminder, you can pass unlimited amounts to your spouse estate tax free.

But you may not want to pass your entire estate to your spouse, as that can conceivably make your surviving spouse's estate too large and cause the beneficiary (s) of the estate unnecessary taxes, as you see in Figure 4.2. In other words, the rule with estates is this: you can leave your estate to your spouse OR you can get an exemption today for FREE from the IRS.

Therefore, the goal is to leave your exempt amount to someone other than your spouse (e.g. children) or you lose it. Because smart attorneys long ago realized that surviving spouses wanted to have this money, yet, also did not want to create a situation where estate taxes would be due, they invented the bypass trust, Figure 4.3

Your exempt amount goes to this trust and your surviving spouse may use it for "health maintenance and welfare." In other words, your spouse can use these funds left in the bypass trusts to maintain his or her standard of living. Once your surviving spouse dies, his or her funds pass to your heirs (e.g. children).

The good news is that at your death, you leave the exempt amount to the bypass trust and these funds are now out of your estate and your spouse's estate. They can grow infinitely and will not be subject to estate tax when they pass to the trust beneficiaries. The attorneys have created a unique planning tool. Your spouse can access the funds if needed, the funds are not counted in the spouse's estate, and you use the exemption that IRA gives to every individual. SO USE IT, or LOSE IT!

So what does this have to do with your IRA?

You may be one of the fortunate few who have the following problem: your retirement funds are such a large part of your estate that in order to pay estate taxes, part of your retirement funds need to be liquidated. For example, you are a married individual with a $7 million estate and $3.5 million of that is an IRA.

First, some good news. You can use your IRA toward your estate exemption. Your beneficiary can be the above mentioned bypass trust. Because it is constructed as a conduit trust for the ultimate beneficiaries who are people (some children are people), those beneficiaries get the benefit of the lifetime stretch. The bypass trust simply takes the annual required minimum distribution from the IRA and distributes it to the beneficiaries. Because the trust distributes all of its income, it pays no tax. So your situation is now the following (using 2009 figures):

- $3.5 million of IRA left to bypass trust and exempt from estate tax.

- $3.5 million of other assets owned by surviving spouse.

- When the surviving spouse dies, assuming the estate does not grow, all of the assets will be exempt and this family will have no estate taxes due.

Figure 4.1: Typical Estate Division: Estate Plan Example Family Assets:

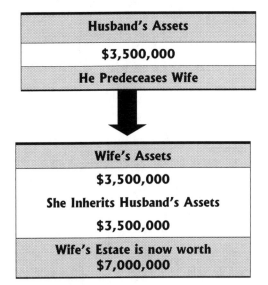

Husband's Assets
$3,500,000
He Predeceases Wife

Wife's Assets
$3,500,000
She Inherits Husband's Assets
$3,500,000
Wife's Estate is now worth $7,000,000

Figure 4.2: Delay Problem to Wife's Death

Wife's Estate	$7,000,000
Tax Exempt Amount	$3,500,000
Taxable Amount	$3,500,000
Estate Taxes	$1,610,000

Figure 4.3: Proper Division Through Credit Shelter Trust

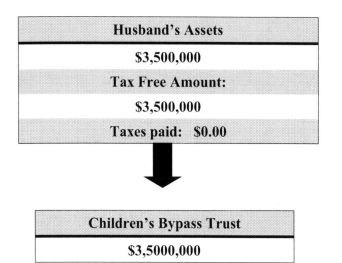

Husband's Assets
$3,500,000
Tax Free Amount:
$3,500,000
Taxes paid: $0.00

Children's Bypass Trust
$3,5000,000

Wife's Assets
$3,500,000
Estate Tax due at time of Death:
$0.00
Taxes paid by Family :
$0.00

USE IT OR LOSE IT!

The basic idea is to make sure that each spouse fully uses his or her estate tax exemption (often called unified credit). These are the amounts under the current tax law:

Table 4.4 Applicable Exemption Per Year

Year Presented	Applicable Exclusion Amount :
2006, 2007, & 2008	2,000,000
2007	2,000,000
2008	2,000,000
2009	3,500,000
2010	**Unlimited**
2011	1,000,000

Under current law, 2010 is scheduled to have an unlimited exemption, therefore you should have no estate tax, and then it returns again in 2011 with a $1 million exemption per person. Of course, this is all subject to modification, as Congress changes tax rates with some frequency. This estate tax roller coaster is sure to slip off the track, so plan on reviewing each estate plan at least each year over the next three years.

Based on this fundamental understanding, you see why it may not be a good idea to die rich. If you have a large retirement plan, it could be subject to both income tax (up to 35% federal plus state income tax) and estate tax (45% in 2009 and 55% in 2011). But if you've stayed awake this far, the solution has occurred to you. Are you thinking of giving away your assets to offset this problem?

What is the Gift Tax?

The Congress thought about this solution and they enacted the gift tax rules. Essentially, the gift tax rules limit the amount of gifts you can give annually and over your lifetime. If you exceed these limits, the giver pays the tax. The recipient pays no taxes on gifts received.

This year, you may give $13,000 (gift tax annual exclusion) to each donee. Your spouse may also give $13,000 to the same donee. You can give more, but then you start using up that 1,000,000 lifetime gift exemption we talked about in the last section, also shown in the table below. But if you want to start using your exclusion during your lifetime, it's a little more restrictive as per the gift tax table:

4.5 Exemption Table

Year	Exemption
2006, 2007, and 2008	1,000,000
2009	1,000,000

Example:

Charlie and his wife, Helen, want to start to give gifts of assets to their nieces and nephews to see what or how they can manage money. Their fear is when they die, the inheritance they will be given may be spent unwisely. So giving some of money today will give insight to Charlie and Helen on how the family does with small gifts while they are still alive and well. Both figure if the family members show irresponsibility with small amounts of money, then maybe a trust is something they may want to consider.

Helen, agrees to split the gifts that they made during 2009. Charlie gives his nephew, George, $21,000, and Helen gives her niece, Gina, $18,000. Although each gift is more than the annual exclusion ($13,000), by gift splitting they can make these gifts without making a taxable gift. Charlie's gift to George is treated as one-half ($10,500) from Charlie and one-half ($10,500)

Helen. Her gift to Gina is also treated as one-half ($9,000) from her and one-half ($9,000) from Charlie. In each case, because one-half of the split gift is not more than the annual exclusion, it is not a taxable gift. However, each of them must file a gift tax return and notify IRS that they have elected gift splitting.

As we proceed through this chapter on leaving retirement assets to heirs, we will re-visit estate taxes because they can be such a large cost when planning for distributions. My experience has shown activating transactions that help you avoid taxes, will create a limit on your wealth potential, while taking an energetic part in strategies that help you recover cost of a tax, will bring additional wealth.

Problems With Custodians:

I think that few financial advisors discuss this with their clients or even understand some of these issues. The custodian that holds your IRA (bank, securities firm, insurance company) may have rules that do not agree with your desires for distributing your IRA. And their rules rule, most of the time!

Let's consider some examples:

*Let's say you have two sons, Jack and Tom. You open a retirement account and come to the part where you complete the beneficiary form. The first line asks for your primary beneficiaries. You list Jack and Tom. Both sons each have a son. Jack's son is Bob. Tom's son is Dan. The next section on the form usually asks for contingent beneficiaries or secondary beneficiaries. You name Bob and Dan (grandsons) as the secondary beneficiaries (A-next page). Here's my question to you. If Jack dies before you, (B-next page) what happens to Jack's half of your IRA when you pass away? You might think that Jack's share would go to his son Bob. **Not always**. Because on your beneficiary form there may not be a place to specify that Bob is Jack's son. **I want to point out to you, that some beneficiary forms are deficient in terms when it come to carrying out half of***

You might think that Jack's share would go to his son Bob, making this is a very simple example, right? Two sons, two grandsons. Unfortunately, this may not be the case. Every custodian has a preset policy for these situations. They will either make the distribution **"per stirpes" (C)** *which will then make Bob your son's decedent beneficiary to his share or* **"per capita" (D)** *the other primary beneficiary. Tom would become the sole beneficiary to the entire account. He in turn could then name his son, Dan, to inherit the money when he dies. Then Bob would be left wondering what Grandpa was thinking.*

Figure 4.6: Beneficiary Designation Issues

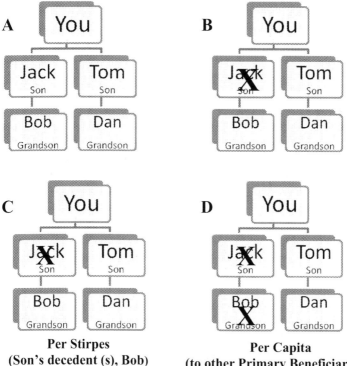

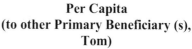

Per Stirpes
(Son's decedent (s), Bob)

Per Capita
(to other Primary Beneficiary (s), Tom)

IRA Misfortune 101

I have been told by many they just write a note and send to the custodian about their desires. ***Don't do that*** and assume they will read it or follow it. Unless you have a friendly custodian that uses the "per stirpes" designation method. The only way to be sure that the custodian follows your desires is through an IRA Asset Will, or by making your beneficiary a trust.

An IRA Asset Will, separate and entirely different than your regular will, is a document that an attorney constructs to replace the one page form that many custodians have. This custom document explains how you desire your IRA to be distributed. However, the custodian is under no obligation to take your IRA asset will. They could tell you "here's OUR form, take it or leave it." And of course, since this is America, the land of choice, you can take your IRA to another custodian, even if you have an inherited IRA. There is another solution. You can name a trust as your IRA beneficiary, we look at that later in this chapter (page 101).

IRA Asset Wills

Funds in your IRAs pass outside of your will, and are distributed according to beneficiary-designation forms that you fill out when you open the accounts. But unlike wills that provide details on how property should be distributed, these forms generally require that account owners name a primary and a secondary beneficiary. Other than that, the custodial institution's policy, not your objectives, will determine how funds get paid out to your heirs. Therefore, what could be your largest financial asset is covered only by a simple, one-page document that may not come close to expressing your intentions about who should inherit the retirement funds you worked so hard to acquire.

Suppose you are single with three grown children (Manny, Moe, Max). You named each an equal beneficiary on your $1 million IRA. Manny dies. Shortly thereafter, you die. The custodian's policy (per capita)(see diagram below) is that Moe and Max will inherit Manny's share of $333,334. Instantly Manny's kids, your 6 grandchildren, were disinherited without a sole knowing about it. Well, the grandkids will find out shortly. But maybe that's not what you wanted.

.

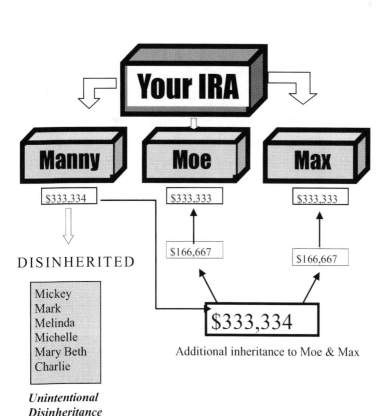

DISINHERITED

Additional inheritance to Moe & Max

Unintentional
Disinheritance

IRA Misfortune 101

You loved those grandkids, especially that oddball Charlie, probably more than the kids, and wanted them to get their father's share.

An IRA Asset Will could have prevented that from happening in that it gives IRA owners the ability to spell out in greater detail what they want to become of their accounts. They can also specify the rights of beneficiaries. For instance, they could include stipulations that beneficiaries will be able to remove more than the minimum required distributions, transfer money to another institution, or divide an account left to several co-beneficiaries as a way to expand the stretch. Most attorneys can prepare the document.

After the document is completed, you need to submit it to the custodian for signature. A number, however, will not unconditionally accept the forms. Some may request a disclaimer promising not to hold them responsible. Others may allow it, but only if the document does not conflict with the terms of their custodial agreement. Often, though, it depends on how persuasive you are and the size of the account.

Here is another potential problem. Some qualified plan custodians may have a forced payoff schedule. A "qualified" plan is a plan through your employer (401(k), profit sharing, pension, defined benefit, etc).

If you have money with an employer's plan and now after all these years of making contributions, you decide to read the fine print. It might say to the effect that, "We don't care who you leave your money to and what age they are, we are going to pay all the money out within five years regardless of the IRS rules that allow for distribution stretching." Although this is not always the case, it does occur sometimes. Typically, the plan's restrictions affect only non-spouse beneficiaries, because your spouse can always roll over your qualified plan money into his or her own IRA and have other options. But before you forget about this paragraph, consider what happens if your spouse predeceases you. Then your primary beneficiary may be a non-spouse and the idea of stretching your retirement money over his or her lifetime could be lost. The solution? Don't leave money in your ex-employers plan—roll it to an IRA. One downside to this may be credit and bankruptcy issues. We cover some information on this topic at the end of this chapter.

> **Do you insist on leaving your money in your "limited investment" 401(k) or profit sharing plan? Like IRA custodians, they too have their own rules that limit your beneficiaries flexibility and tax benefits.**

Yikes—Look at the Taxes!

"Once thought to be relatively obscure, IRD deductions are becoming more common. Big-ticket IRD items such as distributions from IRAs, 401(k)s, 403(b)s, and other tax-sheltered retirement plans of affluent baby boomers have been growing in past decades and will be worth millions when owners bequeath them to estate beneficiaries. Distributions from these plans constitute gross income to the beneficiary and could be subject to marginal federal income tax rates as high as 35%. Plan balances also are subject to estate tax rates as high as 45% in 2009 going to 55% in 2011—a double whammy. Together, these taxes can severely reduce the size of a beneficiary's inheritance."

Journal of Accountancy, April 2004, "Importance of IRD: greater diligence can help CPAs avoid costly tax return omissions."

As most of us know, retirement accounts are all too common to every American. It may seem crazy, but a large IRA could be subject to over a very large part of the IRA.

Example

> *Mr. Smith is widowed and has a net $4 million estate of which $1 million is an IRA; balance consists of raw land, commercial real estate, very little liquidity. His wife had passed, unable to find the time to change the beneficiary, at this point, his estate will inherit his IRA. He is in the 35% federal income tax bracket, 5% net state income tax, and in the 2009 a 45% estate tax bracket. Taxes on his IRA are as follows:*

2009 Tax Year	*2011 Tax Year*
62% Of IRA Value	*100% of IRA Value plus, will need to liquidate other assets.*

(see table on following page)

Federal Income Tax:	*$350,000*	*Federal Income Tax:*	*$350,000*
State Income Tax:	*$50,000*	*State Income Tax:*	*$50,000*
Federal Estate Tax:	*$225,000*	*Federal Estate Tax:*	*$1,650,000*
Total:	***$625,000***	*Total:*	***$2,050,000***

"Wait a minute," you say! "That person does not really have an IRA of $1 million. Since he owes federal income tax at his death, why should he pay estate tax on something he really just owes to the government? That IRA, as far as the federal government is concerned, really only has a value of $375,000 ($1 million less taxes of $625,000)." Right you are. Even Congress has a heart and does not think it's right for people to pay estate tax on an amount that remains in their estate and is really accumulated income tax. So the tax code provides a deduction to the beneficiaries that will inherit the IRA. It's called the deduction for income in respect of a decedent (IRD).

Here's how it works in simplified manner. Each time the beneficiaries receive a distribution from the IRA, they will be entitled to also take a tax deduction equal to 45% (2009) of each payment. In effect, this deduction allows them to re-cover the estate tax paid on the accumulated federal income tax on the decedent's IRA.

While it's true that the IRA beneficiaries will qualify for recovery of the estate tax paid through the IRD Deduction (IRD), this tax deduction could be lost if:

- The beneficiaries don't know to claim it.

- They don't itemize deductions on their personal tax returns.

Therefore, the IRA in the above example is assessed with a 62% tax with possibly no offsets. Can this heavy tax be avoided? Yes. Estate taxes are always voluntary (one can gift the taxable portion of their estate to charity and pay no estate tax) or heavy taxes can be offset by life insurance as we will see later.

IRA Misfortune 101

This situation is the worst possible situation as the IRA owner has named his estate as beneficiary, causing income taxes to be due sooner. By properly naming beneficiaries, the income tax could have been deferred for many years.

Properly Naming Beneficiaries:

The Stretch IRA

The Stretch IRA is not an IRS term, nor is it as mandated law, it is term created by the financial institutions and probably advisors your should avoid. The basic idea is to set up the ability of the named beneficiary (s) to spread required post-death distributions over their life expectancy according to the IRS Single Life Expectancy table. Simply put, it means that someone inheriting an IRA does not need to cash it in and pay the tax at once, but is entitled to take distributions over their life expectancy (and thereby spread the income taxes over several years), per the Table 4.7 (pages 90-91). IRA owners just need to name an individual beneficiary on the IRA to provide the possibility of this lifetime stretch of payments.

Example:

Mr. Eyeawanna Stretch died in 2009. He had named his 40 year old daughter, Wantitall, the sole beneficiary of his IRA. Wantitall will use her 43.6-year life expectancy (see Table 4.7 :pgs 90-91) to determine the required distribution. She only needs to do this once. For each succeeding year, she simply subtracts one from the life expectancy. In this case, the required distribution for 2010 (her second distribution year) would be calculated using a 42.6-year life expectancy. For the third year, the life expectancy would be 41.6years, then 40.6 years,

39.6years, and so on until the original 43.6-year term has expired, unless she withdrawals the IRA before that time, which Wantitall may want to do.

If the IRA owner had named his spouse as beneficiary, the above situation would work differently. Only a spouse beneficiary who is the sole inheritor can go back to this table each year for recalculating life expectancy. A non-spouse beneficiary cannot recalculate, and would only use this table to compute the first year's required distribution for the inherited IRA. The life expectancy will then be reduced by one year for each succeeding year.

In fact, a spouse beneficiary has other options, which we will see when we discuss that circumstance a little later.

THINK ABOUT IT: In the IRS Publication 590: The IRS describes an Individual Retirement Account (IRA) as follows: An individual retirement account is a trust or custodial account set up in the United States for the exclusive benefit of you or your beneficiaries.

IS IT JUST ME: Trust income tax brackets reach max 35% at just $11,150 of income, while ordinary income tax brackets max at $372,950 for married filing jointly. It makes me wonder why the IRS is allowing these retirement trust accounts the benefit of not following trust income tax rates. Is it possible the IRS could turn that switch anytime they want?

Table 4.7
Single Life Expectancy Table (for Inherited IRAs)
(For calculating post-death required distributions to beneficiaries)

Age of IRA Plan	Life Expectancy (in Years)	Age of IRA Plan	Life Expectancy (in Years)	Age of IRA Plan	Life Expectancy (in Years)
0	82.4	24	59.1	48	36.0
1	81.6	25	58.2	49	35.1
2	80.6	26	57.2	50	34.2
3	79.7	27	56.2	51	33.3
4	78.7	28	55.3	52	32.3
5	77.7	29	54.3	53	31.4
6	76.7	30	53.3.	54	30.5
7	75.8	31	52.4	55	29.6
8	74.8	32	51.4	56	28.7
9	73.8	33	50.4	57	27.9
10	72.8	34	49.4	58	27.0
11	71.8	35	48.5	59	26.1
12	70.8	36	47.5	60	25.2
13	69.9	37	46.5	61	24.4
14	68.9	38	45.6	62	23.5
15	67.9	39	44.6	63	22.7
16	66.9	40	43.6	64	21.8
17	66.0	41	42.7	65	21.0
18	65.0	42	41.7	66	20.2
19	64.0	43	40.7	67	19.4
20	63.0	44	39.8	68	18.6
21	62.1	45	38.8	69	17.8
22	61.1	46	37.9	70	17.0
23	60.1	47	37.0	71	16.3

Cont'd

Age of IRA Plan Beneficiary	Life Expectancy (in Years)	Age of IRA Plan Beneficiary	Life Expectancy (in Years)	Age of IRA Plan Beneficiary	Life Expectancy (in Years)
72	15.5	84	8.1	94	4.3
73	14.8	85	7.6	96	3.8
74	14.1	86	7.1	97	3.6
75	13.4	87	6.7	98	3.4
76	12.7	88	6.3	99	3.1
77	12.1	89	5.9	100	2.9
78	11.4	90	5.5	101	2.7
79	10.8	91	5.2	102	2.5
80	10.2	92	4.9	103	2.3
81	9.7	93	4.6	104	2.1
82	9.1	94	4.3	105	1.9
83	8.6	95	4.1	106	1.7

NOTE: Use this table to calculate post death distributions for every designated beneficiary. A non-spouse beneficiary can use this table to calculate the first year required distribution for an inherited IRA. The life expectancy will then be reduced by one for each succeeding year . A spousal beneficiary, who is the soul beneficiary, can use this table each year to re-calculate for life expectancy. DO NOT USE this table to calculate IRA owner's RMD's. See table 3.1 on page 55.

Titling of Inherited IRAs

Given that you're reading this book and you may not be a CPA or financial advisor, it indicates that you have a strange reading list and may have read other items on income taxes. If so, you have encountered one of IRS principals, "substance over form." This is a principal that the IRS uses when a taxpayer does everything by the book but in fact exploits the tax rules to save money. IRS can charge that the true substance of the transaction was to evade taxes.

IRA Misfortune 101

Here's a place where the IRS says its form over substance. Even though the IRA beneficiary may intend to stretch IRA distributions over his lifetime, and does so using the proper distribution tables and taking timely annual distributions, if the IRA is titled incorrectly, IRS will declare the entire account as distributed and require all taxes.

Before a non-spouse beneficiary starts requirement minimum distributions (RMDs), the IRA must be titled correctly. Each beneficiary's share of the IRA should be kept separate and the Social Security number changed as soon as possible after the owner's death. However, the deceased owner's name must remain on the account. If non-spouse beneficiaries re-title the account to their own name the funds become immediately taxable.

In the above case, the IRA could be re-titled as: Eyeawanna Stretch IRA (deceased January 10, 2009) F/B/O (for benefit of), Want-it-all Stretch. Where there is more than one beneficiary, each would have his or her own F/B/O account.

Every beneficiary should name a beneficiary as soon as he or she inherits an IRA so that there will be someone to continue the payout schedule if the beneficiary dies. This will also avoid probate and other will-related problems. If the beneficiary names a beneficiary, the remaining IRA balance will go directly to that beneficiary with no probate, claims, or other legal obstacles.

In the above case, if Wantitall dies before her 43.6-year term has expired and there is still a balance in the IRA, then her beneficiary (assumption that one was added) can continue the remaining years left on Wantitall's original 43.6-year schedule.

Non-Spouse Beneficiaries Issues

Prior to 2006, non-spouse beneficiaries were not allowed to do IRA rollovers as per IRC Section 408(d)(3)(C), and they could not use the 60-day rollover rule. The Pension Protection Act of 2006 first enacted what we thought was the ability for non-spouse beneficiary rollovers. But the details provided otherwise.

Congress just fixed this problem with a technical correction to the P.P.A. 2006. However this correction will not take effect until 2010.

Most employer plans do not allow the beneficiaries the opportunity to create a Stretch IRA. This will now allow a non-spouse beneficiary to do a direct rollover of inherited plan assets to a properly titled inherited IRA. The plan participant requirement is that he died in 2006 or later.

IRA beneficiaries are not permitted to convert inherited IRAs, (IRS notice 2008-30 March 2008), yet, those who inherit from a company plan can convert their inherited balances. In addition, if the plan participant dies this year (2009), then when 2010 rolls around the plan must offer the post-death transfer to an inherited IRA, and thanks to The Tax Prevention & Reconciliation Act of 2006, in the year 2010 plan beneficiaries qualify to complete a Roth IRA conversion. The tax will need to be paid on the conversion.

Communication Quick Points:

I.   Recovery Act 2008 announced that non-spouse beneficiary transfer from employer plans, like a 401K, will be mandatory beginning in 2010.

II. In 2010 non-spouse beneficiaries can convert their inherited company plan assets to inherited Roth IRAs. In addition they can spread the income over two tax years. IRA to ROTH IRA conversion in 2010, pay first tax payment 2011, Second tax payment 2012. In effect, making the first tax installment 18 months after the conversion, (April 15, 2011).

III. IRS Notice 2008-30 issued March 5, 2008 & TIPRA of 2006 added benefits.

IV. Consider applying the cost of conversion tax (lost opportunity cost) as discussed in Chapter 2.

Non-spouse Roth IRA beneficiaries must take required distributions. But generally they will be tax-free.

The cost basis of an IRA carries to all beneficiaries. If the contributions were tax deductible, all withdrawals are taxable to the beneficiaries. However, if the deceased owner had made non-deductible contributions, those contributions become the cost basis. Thus, there is no tax on those amounts. But most beneficiaries do not realize this, and end up paying more tax than necessary.

You will have to locate Form 8606, which shows the amount of non-deductible IRA contributions. This will be attached to the decedent's past tax returns. But just because you can't find any copies of Form 8606 does not mean there weren't any non-deductible contributions made. Possibly, they just weren't filed.

Check IRA statements, or find IRS Form 5498, which shows if IRA contributions were made. You can then refer to the tax return to see if a deduction was made. If it wasn't, you can assume that the contribution was nondeductible.

Inherited Roth IRAs are much simpler since all the contributions were non-deductible, and can be taken out tax-free. Furthermore, the earnings can also be distributed tax-free as long as the Roth was held for more than five years (including the time held by the original owner). However, if you fail to take required distributions from the inherited Roth IRAs, you get hit with a 50% penalty on the amount not taken.

Separate Account for Non-Spouse Beneficiaries

There are non-tax reasons to create separate trusts for beneficiaries:

- Individual life expectancies can be used.
- Avoid beneficiary disagreements.
- Maintain separate investment strategies by beneficiary.
- Beneficiaries have option to choose separate IRA custodians.
- Special needs of certain beneficiaries.

The question is, if you have three beneficiaries, should you divide your IRA into three accounts now, or allow it to be handled post death? Unless you like getting three statements and needing to make three transactions every time you want to make a change to your IRA, just make sure that the parties involved understand that the account should be divided later.

In most cases, it would be best that each beneficiary be able to use his or her own age for computing the RMD on the inherited IRA. This way if one beneficiary is 20 years old and another beneficiary is 50 years old, the 20 year old would not be forced to use the life expectancy of a 50 year old. Separate beneficiary can be created after the death of the IRA owner to solve this problem.

Beneficiaries have until December 31 of the year following the year of the IRA owner's death to split the inherited IRA and create separate accounts.

But there is another rule that states that the identity of the designated beneficiary for calculating post-death RMDs is determined on September 30 of the year following the year of the IRA owner's death. If at September 30 of the year following the year of the IRA owner's death, there are still three beneficiaries on the IRA, then it would seem that the designated beneficiary would be the oldest or the one with the shortest life expectancy, or there would be no designated beneficiary if one of the three beneficiaries was an estate or a charity.

The regulations, however, do not require the IRA to actually be split until December 31 of the year following the year of the IRA owner's death. This means that if an IRA owner names three children as co-beneficiaries on an IRA, they can each still be the designated beneficiaries on their separate shares if the account is split after the September 30 beneficiary designation date but before the end of the year.

For example, if the IRA owner died in 2008, separate shares for RMD purposes can be created even if the account is split after September 30, 2009, as long as the IRA is split by December 31, 2009. Does this mean that the designated beneficiary can be determined as late as December 31 of the year following the year of death? No. The only explanation then, for the two dates is that September 30 is the date that the designated beneficiary is determined and December 31st is merely an administrative date by which the actual split must be done. To be safe they should split by the September 30 date. That still gives the beneficiaries plenty of time.

To add to the confusion, the account technically does not have to be split into several different physical IRAs to create separate shares. If beneficiaries are willing to account for post-death gains and losses on their separated inherited amounts in a single IRA, that could also qualify as creating separate shares without physically splitting the IRA into separate accounts. However, this will create an ongoing paperwork nightmare. If beneficiaries desire separate shares, they should physically split the inherited IRA in a timely fashion.

Spousal Advantages

When it comes to the spouse inheriting the IRA, the spouse gets special flexibility. (This should make you feel good that you'll be dead and your spouse is *still* getting special advantages.)

Only spouses can rollover an inherited IRA into their own IRAs. If the deceased was in the RMD status, the year-of-death distribution must be taken before the rollover is allowed. The funds will then be considered to be the surviving spouse's account subject to the spouse's own age.

- The surviving spouse is not under any obligation to rollover an IRA. It can be done anytime. This allows flexibility for a survivor. The spousal rollover can be accomplished in two ways:

- Withdraw the decedent's IRA and deposit in his or her IRA within 60 days.

- Directly move the funds via a trustee-to-trustee transfer (preferred) surviving spouse under 59½.

IRA Misfortune 101

The spouse may want to retain "beneficiary status" and not rollover the account. When the survivor is under 59 ½ and wants to take out money and avoid the 10% early withdrawal penalty the spouse can do so if he or she is a beneficiary. Why? Because when you are a beneficiary, the age 59 ½ rule does not apply; there is no 10% penalty for taking money from an inherited IRA. However, if the spouse rolled over the IRA to his or her own name, is under 59 ½ and takes distributions, the early withdrawal penalty would apply.

Surviving Spouse Over 59 ½

Assume the IRA owner dies before his RBD at 68, and named his spouse as the IRA beneficiary. The spouse is 65 years old. If the spouse chooses to be a direct beneficiary, she does not have to begin taking distributions until December 31 of the year the IRA owner would have attained age 70½. If the spouse chooses a spousal rollover, the spouse treats it as her own IRA, and would not have to begin taking distributions until after she attains age 70½. In most cases, it would be beneficial to use the spousal rollover.

Surviving Spouse Older Than Deceased

It might pay to use the beneficiary route if the surviving spouse was much older, for example, 75 years old, and the retirement plan owner was much younger, say 65. In this case, if the surviving spouse chose to be a beneficiary, he or she would not have to start drawing until the year the retirement plan owner would have attained age 70½. In this case, even though the surviving spouse is 75 years old, he or she may not have to draw down for another five years, as opposed to choosing the spousal rollover, which would mean the spouse would have to begin withdrawals by December 31 of the year following death.

If the spouse is named as the retirement plan beneficiary, when the retirement plan owner dies, the spouse should immediately name new beneficiaries. If the surviving spouse dies before doing so, the beneficiary will generally be the estate and then all chances of extending the life expectancy by naming younger beneficiaries will be lost.

No Beneficiary

Suppose that the owner of an IRA or company plan dies before his or her RBD without naming a designated beneficiary?

The beneficiaries must then withdraw from the account under the five-year rule. And it does not matter how much they take out during the five-year rule period, as long as the account is depleted by December 31 of the fifth year after owner's death. Any balance remaining is subject to the 50% penalty.

On the other hand, if an account owner dies after the RBD and has no designated beneficiary, then the distribution period is the owner's life expectancy calculated in the year of death, reduced by one for each subsequent year.

The longest possible distribution period for the IRA would then be 15.3 years. For an IRA owner, the RBD is April 1 of the year after he or she turns 70½ , which always falls in the second required distribution year. If the owner turned 70½ years old in 2009, the first distribution year is 2009, but the RBD is April 1, 2010, which is in the second distribution year. Death before that date means the owner died before reaching his RBD, even if he or she had already taken a required distribution.

If the IRA owner has passed the RBD and there is no designated beneficiary, the IRA can be paid out over the remaining single life expectancy of the deceased IRA owner. The longest possible single life expectancy of an IRA owner who has passed his RBD is 16.3 years. That's the life expectancy of a 71-year old.

Distributions to the beneficiary must begin in the year after the IRA owner's death and the factor is reduced by one each year, so the longest possible stretch out is 15.3 years, regardless of who ends up inheriting the IRA. It's true that an IRA owner could be age 70 in the first distribution year, but if he died in that year, he would have died before his RBD and the IRA with no designated beneficiary would have to be paid out under the five year rule.

Example:

An IRA owner is 70 ½ years old in 2008 and for whatever reason has no designated beneficiary. The default language in the IRA custodial document says that at his death the IRA beneficiary is his estate. He dies in June 2009, which is after his RBD of April 1, 2009. If he died in 2008, his first required distribution year, he would have died before his RBD, and with no designated beneficiary, the heirs of his estate would be stuck with the five year payout. Since he died after his RBD, the IRA can be paid out over his remaining single life expectancy of 16.3 years based on his age in the year of death (age 71 in 2009). The first post-death re-quired distribution must be taken by the end of 2010, the year after the IRA owner's death. For the first bene-ficiary distribution, the life expectancy will be 15.3 years (the 16.3 years less one year). The 15.3 years will be reduced by one for each succeeding year .

This example illustrates the longest possible payout after death when there is no designated beneficiary. Most IRAs will be paid out sooner. In case you were wondering, the shortest possible payout with no designated beneficiary is not five years, but can be even less. If the IRA owner died after age 89, the remaining life expectancy would be less than five years. The single life expectancy for an 89 year old is 5.9 years. If he dies at age 89, the remaining payout on the IRA would be only 4.9 years. If he died after reaching 111 years of age, the entire IRA would have to be paid out in the year following the year of the IRA owner's death.

Creating Trusts for IRA

Should I add the complication and cost of a Trust for IRA Beneficiary (s)?

Even though there are no tax benefits, there may be circumstances when you want to name a trust as your IRA beneficiary. Trusts, however, create unique problems and tax complications even when executed perfectly. IRA trusts cannot provide the answers for tax and personal solutions that many IRA owners are seeking. And quite often, trusts are poorly drafted and cause more problems than they are worth.

IRA owners can name trusts as beneficiary as a way to better control post-death distributions, and restrict access for beneficiaries who might otherwise squander large inherited IRAs. Alternatively, adult beneficiaries may need help with managing the IRA funds and taking required distributions. They simply may lack the necessary financial judgment for larger sums.

IRA Misfortune 101

For the duration of my 25 year career, it appears to me that clients have three general issues. First they want *Control* of this asset, even after the funeral. They seem to want to take advantage of the *Estate Tax Exemption,* and many would like the beneficiaries to take advantage of the *Stretch.*

My clients have told me that the reason they name a trust as beneficiary is not to restrict the beneficiary, but to insure that the IRA funds are protected from creditors and bankruptcy. Since the trust assets are not actually owned by your beneficiary, if your beneficiary is pursued by creditors or succumbs to bankruptcy, the trust assets are protected.

Instead of naming a person (for example a child or grandchild) as a direct beneficiary on the account, a trust would be named. The trust beneficiary would be the child, grandchild, or other person that the IRA owner wants to receive the IRA. Or suppose that you want to control the ultimate disposition of his IRA.

In a typical second marriage (or even with some first marriages), you may want to leave your spouse the annual IRA income, but after survivor's death you want to make sure that the IRA goes to your children and not to those from the spouse's first marriage. A trust can be used to hold money for estate taxes if there is a risk that the IRA beneficiary will take the money and run without paying his share of the estate tax.

When an individual is a direct beneficiary of an IRA, the entire IRA goes to that person at death. There is usually a clause in the will called the "tax apportionment clause," which spells out who is responsible for the estate tax, both on items that pass through the will, and on property that passes outside, is lost to the ultimate beneficiaries, the will, such as an IRA or life insurance. But even if the will's tax clause states that the IRA beneficiary must pay his or her share of the estate tax from the IRA proceeds, it may be too late if the beneficiary has already fled with the newly inherited funds. A trust could escrow a portion of the IRA for estate taxes. This would not apply to a non-taxable estate, where assets are under the limits shown in the Appendix.

A feature of trusts, is that you bring another party into the equation, the trustee, to act on behalf of the beneficiary. The trustee may be a trusted family member, a bank that accepts fiduciary responsibilities or an advisor that will make sound business decisions on behalf of the beneficiary.

If the trust is appropriate, it must qualify under the various IRS rules in order for the trust beneficiaries to be able to use their own life expectancies for calculating post-death required distributions. If the trust does not qualify as a designated beneficiary the stretch IRA possibility is lost.

The requirements for a trust to qualify as a designated beneficiary are:[8]

- The trust must be a valid trust under state law.
- The trust must be irrevocable at death.
- The beneficiaries of the trust must be identifiable.
- A copy of the trust document must be provided to the plan by October 31 of the year following the year of the IRA owner's death.

---

[8] IRSP.R. §1.401(a)(9)-4,A-5

- The beneficiaries of the trust must be individuals.
- No person may have the power to change the beneficiaries after December 31 of the year after the participant's death.

If these requirements are met, then the trust qualifies as a designated beneficiary, and the trust beneficiary's life expectancy can be used to calculate post-death required minimum distributions. If the trust fails to qualify, then there is no designated beneficiary and trust beneficiaries will not be able to stretch post-death required distributions over their life expectancies. In that case, the IRA will be paid out either under the five-year rule (if the IRA owner dies before his Required Beginning Date) or over the remaining life expectancy of the deceased IRA owner (if the IRA owner dies after his RBD).

The arguments against using a trust are as follows:
- Adds more complication.
- Most beneficiary planning can be accomplished through comprehensive designation planning.
- Additional tax return to be filed creates annual cost.
- Initial cost of trust, amended trust costs, opportunity costs.

If there are multiple beneficiaries, they must all use the life expectancy of the beneficiary who is oldest. If you have three children close in age, it does not have much impact on their respective stretch periods. However, if the beneficiaries have large differences in age, you should use a trust for each.

Let's go back to what clients seem to want, for instance, you come into my office and say:

I want The **Estate Tax Exemption** and the **Control**. Well that's very simple, leave the IRA to a Credit Shelter Trust. You get the estate tax exemption, you get control, your bride normally benefits from the trust.

Now you change your mind and say:

*"I want the **Stretch** and the I want **Control**." Fill out the primary designation on the beneficiary form and leave the IRA to your bride.*

You get control and when you die, your spouse names the kids as the primary beneficiary. One small problem leaving all to the spouse, this method blows the estate tax exemption.

I know your smart, because your reading my book. You recall the section on disclaiming an IRA, so your bride realizes she doesn't need the money and there is going to be an estate tax problem. She hears you yelling from the grave, "Call Tim, and ask him what to do." I say, "Disclaim the money and allow your contingent beneficiary to receive the money." I am confident that you did a magnificent job filling in the contingent beneficiary area to give passage and allow a disclaim.

What's that, now you decide you want The **Estate Tax Exemption** and the **Stretch**? Complete a beneficiary designation form and leave it to the kids, list your bride as contingent beneficiary. Only problem with this, is your bride may need or want some money at your death. A simple solution is to replace it with life insurance. I know, all those T.V. Guru's told you to go out and buy term insurance when you were young, because no idiot needs life insurance when you are retired, because your house is paid off and the kids are gone. **Oops, Wonder how those advisors feel about the litigation process!**

Its impossible to have all three wants, unless you own permanent life insurance equal to your estate, this will allow you to have all three, the estate tax exemption, control and the stretch.

Naming a Charity as Beneficiary

I want to make my charities a benefactor to half of my estate, Is this good judgment?

Many people think of leaving this money in checking accounts because for years they have issued checks to these charities from this account. You may think that it's a nice thing to leave half of your estate by choosing this asset to give. Review some quick thoughts on this.

Let's assume you die with $200,000 - $100,000 in your IRA, and $100,000 in your checking account. Do you think your heirs, (by the way are very successful high tax bracket citizens) would rather inherit the checking account money or the IRA money? Leaving the IRA to your favorite Charity will not cost them or your estate one tax dollar. The charity receives $100,000; the charity is a non taxable entity. If you leave the heirs a $100,000 from your IRA and they have to pay tax, they will net much less cash, up to 35% less ($65,000). If you leave them your checking accounts, the heirs get 100% of the asset, no tax.

When one of your IRA beneficiaries is a charity, it's even more important to split the IRA for multiple beneficiaries as we discussed previously. Since a charity has no life expectancy, if your IRA is not split among your beneficiaries, they will all be subject to drain the IRA based on the beneficiary with the shortest life expectancy (in this case zero) and be stuck with the five year rule.

Why it's not only those over 70½ who are at risk

Retirees of any age with large IRAs must understand that their IRAs can be hit with estate and income taxes when they die. And RMD rules could cause future income tax burdens while they are alive. However, IRA owners between ages 59½ and 70½ have a great opportunity to use current tax law to their advantage, 'cause folks it's going to change. I mean change big time!

If they are in lower tax brackets (10% or 15%), they can remove just enough money from their IRAs to use up those brackets. When they turn 70½, they will have reduced the amount subject to RMD. Their future tax brackets may be lowered because of smaller withdrawals, and they will have shifted more of their assets out of their IRA. In addition, most assets held outside an IRA pass income-tax-free to beneficiaries. If your tax preparer doesn't bring this to your attention or review this with you each year from 59½ to 70½, do the Donald Trump thing, **fire him/her immediately.**

Protect the IRA Value
Life insurance

Earlier, we showed how a large IRA in a significant estate can be burdened with an 86% combined tax (federal income tax, state income tax and state estate tax). A common way to offset these taxes is by using life insurance. Since these taxes are due or become liabilities at death, and life insurance pays at death, the tax liability and the life insurance death benefit are perfectly matched in time.

IRA Misfortune 101

Note that when spouses inherit IRAs and any other asset, they defer the estate tax on the accounts because of the unlimited marital deduction. However, they will still have to pay income tax on distributions that must begin when they reach age 70½, and there may still be estate taxes due at death of the survivor. Too many people stop doing planning after one spouse dies. This is the time to step up, raise the bar for perfection with an estate plan!

Life insurance is the most efficient way to protect a large IRA. Non-IRA assets that are creating additional tax cost should be used first to buy the insurance. However, even if you need to remove money from the IRA to pay the premiums, the life insurance scenario may still be beneficial as in the example above. And if the IRA owner is over 70½, he or she needs to begin Required Minimum Distributions (RMD). So why not leverage the distribution and own permanent life insurance?

I get nervous when advisors push people to place life insurance policies into an irrevocable life insurance trust. This transaction should only take place as a last item on the checklist. I have reviewed many plans of individuals seeking protection methods for IRA assets. Only two of those cases had verifiable evidence to support an irrevocable trust. What seems to be the pitch is the fact that when you are the owner of your own life insurance the entire death benefit is included as an estate asset. It is, but so often this is a better strategy with much lower cost than placing this asset in an irrevocable trust.

Many of those cases looked like the example below:

*Buy a life insurance policy on the husband for $1
Million; the premium is $24,000 for a 60 year old. So they
don't pay an estate tax on the million. The recommendation
is to place the policy in an irrevocable life insurance trust.
The premiums will be paid by taking your money and gifting
it to the two kids (beneficiaries). Each child will receive
$12,000 to pay half of the premium. The common concern
noted from these advisors is the million left inside your estate
will cause 46% estate tax cost. However, this is easily
avoided by owning the policy outside of your estate.*

**Follow their notes! You use the $12,000 annual gift
exclusion as follows:**

- **You establish an irrevocable life insurance trust (ILIT)—
any estate planning attorney can draw this document.**

- **You appoint a trustee of the trust (a trusted family
member or advisor).**

- **You decide on the beneficiaries of the trust (e.g. your
two children).**

- **You gift to the trust the amount needed to pay the
annual life insurance premium. Let's assume it's
$24,000. You gift to the trust $24,000, $12,000 on
behalf of each of the two beneficiaries (gifts of
$12,000 per donee per year are not subject to gift taxes
so you're clear, max in 2009 is $13,000 per individual
or entity).**

- **The trustee takes the cash and pays the premium,
and the owner of the policy is the ILIT. The policy is out
of your estate and will never be subject to estate taxes.**

This will keep the death proceeds out of the IRA owner's estate. When the owner dies, the life insurance proceeds will be used to pay the estate tax (or any way that the beneficiaries desire), thus the beneficiaries will not have to invade the IRA to pay taxes. The beneficiaries will then be able to stretch out the IRA withdrawals and the income tax over a period of many years.

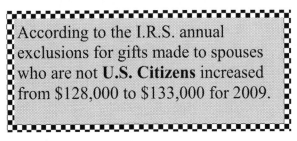

According to the I.R.S. annual exclusions for gifts made to spouses who are not **U.S. Citizens** increased from $128,000 to $133,000 for 2009.

Let's study this transaction:

Life expectancy for Male age 60 is 81

Life expectancy for Female age 60 is 84

Two million dollar taxable estate today has a projected value at age 81 of $6,800,000, subtract those premiums going to the trust, the estate value estimates to $5,700,000, 46% estate tax cost 2.6 million. I think that million is going to be short of tax due.

Money taken from estate, $24,000 for 21 years @ 6% cost of money is over $1,000,000. You have paid part of the estate tax with your cash and decreased, your estate, and maybe you will experience quality of life issues.

- Irrevocable life insurance policy cash values can not be used by client.
- Tax Laws change, no way to recover this massive cost!

- Must die early for plan to be efficient.

- Legal fees initially, maybe annually to review plan.

- Accounting fees for trust, annually.

- Is this really what you wanted!

*NOTE: If you have bought, or are in the process, of buying life insurance and placing it in an irrevocable trust, **STOP!** Call my office immediately; I will do everything in my control to alter my schedule to see you immediately. That's how important this is, folks. This might very well be the largest and most costly mistake of your life.*

IRAs—The Missing Link in Many Seniors' Estate Plans

According to the IRS, 43 million people have $17.6 trillion in retirement accounts. Most of this money will become IRA rollovers, and the dollars will continue to grow. Yet IRAs are neglected in the average estate plan because investors do not know they are neglected, sometimes thinking that their IRA plans are handled through their wills or living trusts.

They don't know until you ask them who will inherit their IRA or retirement account. And if not updated, an unintended person, such as an ex-spouse, could get funds that were earmarked for the current spouse because the forms weren't updated.

Why be concerned since the estate tax is supposed to disappear?

That is not a bet you should make. For even if the tax goes away, the income tax "step-up-in-basis" provision for the most part goes away too. And beneficiaries could use life insurance to pay the capital gains tax on appreciated assets rather than liquidate the IRA. They'll then have the opportunity to stretch the distributions out and delay paying the associated income tax on the withdrawals.

They'll then have the opportunity to stretch the distributions out and delay paying the associated income tax on the withdrawals

Therefore, it's better to plan on the probability that the tax will remain because that's a more conservative outlook. The worst scenario might be that there are no taxes to pay, and the beneficiaries inherit more tax-free money.

If the parents want to do the stretch IRA for their beneficiaries, then leaving a large IRA increases the estate size, and they need life insurance to pay the estate tax. If they don't care about the stretch (i.e. they have plenty of other assets to leave the kids or don't care about the kids), then they can buy life insurance with their retirement money.

Example

In this example, the IRA owner of large estate is age 60. He has two choices: allow his IRA to continue to grow or do planning. His estate is subject to the top estate tax bracket in 2006 and he is using current rates for his planning. Assume that the money grows at a hypothetical 8% annually and that he is in good health and insurable. He has a $100,000 IRA and dies ten years from today. Here's what happened under the two scenarios of do no planning or add life insurance to the plan.

In the illustration (Table 4.8), the beneficiaries would lose $99,311 to estate taxes if the IRA owner keeps the IRA and dies in ten years. The inheritance will be further diminished by the beneficiaries' personal income tax rates. An alternative would be to start taking IRA distributions at age 60, pay the income tax, and buy a life insurance policy with the after-tax distribution.

The IRA owner could withdraw $6,000 per year and purchase a $ 100,000 life insurance policy. If the IRA owner dies in year ten, his heirs would net $44.854, from the IRA and $ 54,000 from the life insurance. In this example using life insurance created $20,744 in additional wealth. Many professional advisors inform their clients that permanent life insurance cost will create lower wealth. Be aware of this false information

Table 4.8:
Protect an IRA With Life Insurance

	Keep IRA Do NO Planning	Using Life Insurance
$100,000 IRA Balance in 10Yrs 8%	$215,893	$123,973
Estate Tax (46%)	($99,311)	($57,027)
Beneficiary gets	$116,582	$66,946
33% Income tax	($38,472)	($22,092)
Net IRA Proceeds	$78,110	$44,854
Life Insurance Proceeds*	0.00	$100,000
Estate Tax (46%)	0.00	$46,000.
Net Life Insurance Proceeds	0.00	$54,000
Net to Beneficiary	$78,110	$98,854

*A 60-year-old non-smoker, $4,234.00 annual premium for 10 years. Assume life policy is owned by insured. Taxes are combined federal and state. Note that the purchase of life insurance involves underwriting process to qualify for premium rate to determine eligibility.

If the IRA owner dies in year ten, his heirs would net $46,662 from the IRA and $ 100,000 from the life insurance. This transfer could save almost $70,000 on a $100,000 IRA.

Creditors and Bankruptcy

When you hold retirement money in a qualified plan, those assets are protected by the Employee Retirement Income Security Act (ERISA). This is a federal law, so no matter in which of the 50 states you reside, your retirement funds are creditor protected. Notably, this protection applied *only* to ERISA-plan assets—if a retirement plan is not subject to ERISA, it is not excluded or protected. The most common plans not subject to ERISA (and thus not receiving the ERISA-based protection) are traditional, Roth, SEP, and SIMPLE IRAs, and retirement plans for self-employed business owners (for example, individual 401(k)s) where a failure to have any non-owner "employees" meant that ERISA's employee-oriented protections would not apply.

Many states that opted out of the federal exemptions have included IRA accounts in their list of state exemptions, thereby providing partial or full (depending on the state's exact rules) creditor protection for IRAs. But in states that use the federal exemptions, or grant creditors the right to choose federal (instead of state) exemptions, IRAs have been troublesome. In other words, the protection of IRA from creditors or in bankruptcy has been a state-by-state issue.

That changed in 2005, because of a Supreme Court decision in a matter involving IRAs plus the passage of the Bankruptcy Abuse Protection and Consumer Protection Act of 2005 (BAPCPA). Let's look at each of these so you understand the protection you have once you do an IRA rollover from your company plan

The Supreme Court Case

The case focused on an Arkansas couple, Richard and Betty Jo Rousey, who declared bankruptcy in 2001. They were laid off from their jobs at Northrop Grumman and had rolled over their employer retirement accounts into IRAs after leaving the firm. The Rouseys claimed that the $55,000 in their IRAs should be protected from creditors in the bankruptcy proceedings. The court did not agree. Undeterred, the Rouseys, although bankrupt, somehow had enough cash to take their argument to the Supreme Court. The Supreme Court ruled in their favor, stating that their IRAs were protected from creditors.

The Supreme Court evaluated three basic tests under the Bankruptcy Code:

- "The right to receive the payment must be from a stock bonus, pension, profit sharing, annuity, or similar plan or contract."

- "The right to receive payment must be on account of illness, disability, death, age, or length of service."

- "The right to receive payment may be exempted only to the extent that it is reasonably necessary to support the account holder or his dependents."

The court held that the first provision was satisfied—IRAs "have the same primary purpose, namely, to enable Americans to save for their retirement" and, like other retirement plans, have a common feature in that "they provide income that substitutes for wages earned as salary or hourly compensation."

On the second test, the court ruled that the right to receive payment from an IRA *is* on account of age, referring both to the 10% early withdrawal penalty applicable to IRAs, as well as the age 70½ required minimum distribution rules (and the associated 50% excise penalty for failure to take withdrawals).

Since both of these 'tests' were satisfied, the Supreme Court ruled in favor of the Rouseys.

The third test was not even presented before the Supreme Court—ultimately, to actually protect their entire account balance the Rouseys will still need to prove how much of the account balance deserves to be protected as reasonably necessary for support. In general, extremely large account balances may still have 'excess' amounts subject to creditors, even with the granted IRA protection. So if your IRA funds are not reasonably necessary for your support (i.e. you have plenty of other assets), then don't rely on this decision. In other words, if you're not reliant on your IRA assets, this decision won't help protect your IRA assets. You may in fact have protection under the federal bankruptcy laws or your state's rules addressed below.

Unfortunately, the protection you have is not always clear. Not all states actually use the federal bankruptcy exemptions. In fact, some states have state-level bankruptcy exemptions. Consequently, in some states, the state's exemptions *must* be used. In other states, individuals have the choice of federal or state exemptions, and only in the remaining states must the federal statutes be used. Consequently, the Supreme Court's decision will only apply in states where the individual has a choice between state and federal exemptions and *chooses* the federal exemptions, or in states where the federal rules *must* apply, such as:

Alaska, Arkansas, Connecticut, Hawaii, Michigan, Minnesota, New Hampshire, New Jersey, New Mexico, Pennsylvania, Rhode Island, South Dakota, Texas, Vermont, Washington, Wisconsin, and the District of Columbia.

ERISA protection provided money in a qualified plan (401(k), etc) universally pre-empts state law, and always provides creditor protection. It's also unclear whether the ruling will apply to Roth IRAs, which have far fewer age-based restrictions (since contributions can be withdrawn penalty-free at any time, and no required minimum distributions apply during lifetime). Thus Roth IRAs would not meet the three-prong test evaluated by the Supreme Court.

The protection provided by the Rouseys' case is weak, much weaker than protection provided by ERISA-level, will only apply in a limited number of states, and will *only* apply to the extent reasonably necessary for support (which is still determined by the bankruptcy courts on a case-by-case basis). Consequently, decisions to complete IRA rollovers from ERISA-protected retirement plans must still be made carefully. So be aware that when you roll assets from a company plan to an IRA, you may lose creditor protection. I recommend checking with legal counsel in your state. There seems to be some question with regard to rollover attributable to rollover contributions. I hear often many experts say this phrase should be interpreted to mean that amounts rolled over from your employer plan (i.e.401ᴋ) get creditor protection as well. Others contradict this interpretation. Problem is, court ruling is absent on this issue. I have a hard time convincing myself to leave money in a 401ᴋ account for bankruptcy protection.

The Bankruptcy Law

The Bankruptcy Abuse Protection and Consumer Protection Act of 2005 (BAPCPA) simultaneously increased, in some cases substantially, the creditor protection available to retirement accounts for those who declare bankruptcy.

Before implementation of the Bankruptcy Act, the protection of retirement accounts from creditors during bankruptcy had been subject to multiple rules depending on the type of account and the applicable state. Employer retirement plans received creditor protection due to the Employer Retirement Income Security Act of 1974 (ERISA), but only a limited number of retirement account types were actually subject to ERISA.

For non-ERISA-protected plans, protection has varied by state. The extent of relief for debtors with retirement accounts would depend on which bankruptcy protections applied for a particular debtor's state. Protection varied from unlimited in some states to none in others, and professionals, much less retirement plan owners, often had difficulty keeping track of which states applied which protections (keep this in mind if you relocate from one state to another). BAPCPA has simplified retirement account creditor protection by eliminating much of the differentiation among types of plans and bankruptcy jurisdictions.

Basic Retirement Account Rules Under BAPCPA

Under the new rules of BAPCPA, virtually all types of retirement accounts are now exempt assets in bankruptcy proceedings. This was accomplished by adding a provision creating a new exemption for "retirement funds to the extent that those funds are in a fund or account that is exempt from taxation under Sections 401,403,408,408A, 414,457, or 501(a) of the Internal Revenue Code." This covers 401(k)s, 403(b)s, profit-sharing and money purchase plans, IRAs (including SEP, SIMPLE plans, Roth), as well as defined-benefit plans. (There are limitations as described below). But non-qualified annuities, although tax-deferred and ostensibly for retirement, will not be protected under these provisions since the applicable Section 72 is not listed (although qualified annuities will still be protected under the applicable IRA or qualified plan section). Many states have rules that give protection to nonqualified annuities.

To greatly aid simplification for debtors, the provisions exempting retirement plans of all types were added to the existing code twice—once in the list of federal exemptions, and again as one of the add-ons applicable to all states that opt out for their own state exemptions. Consequently, this blanket protection for all types of retirement accounts applies regardless of whether the debtor is eligible (or required) to use the federal or state exemptions. Because the relevant protection was added in each applicable section of the law, it should apply in either case.

The Problem of Being Too Rich

Unfortunately, although BAPCPA has created an exemption for all types of retirement plans, the exemption for those plans is not unlimited in all cases. The catch is that, in the case of Roth and traditional IRAs, the maximum amount of the exemption is limited to an aggregate IRA account value of $1 million (adjusted every three years for inflation). SEP and SIMPLE IRAs, along with all other types of non-IRA retirement accounts such as 401(k)s and 403(b)s, are not included in determining the $1 million limit—it applies only to traditional and Roth IRAs.

In addition, this $1 million limitation does not include any amounts held in an IRA that are attributable to eligible rollover contributions (and subsequent rollover growth). Eligible rollover contributions are those that occur under a series of explicitly listed Internal Revenue Code rollover provisions. The end result is that rollovers from any qualified employer retirement plan will qualify, but IRA-to-IRA rollovers will not. In other words, if your money was fully protected in a qualified employer plan and rolled over, the bankruptcy law continues to protect it fully as a rollover IRA.

Note that rollovers that did not come from an ERISA plan are protected only up to $1 million. Consequently, a rollover from a SEP or SIMPLE IRA to a traditional IRA would appear to forfeit unlimited protection and potentially subject the assets to the $1 million aggregate traditional and Roth IRA protection cap.

The good news is that, in the foreseeable future, the $1 million limitation is not likely to apply to many taxpayers. Foregoing the issue of rollovers from SEP and SIMPLE IRAs, the only type of IRA account balances that would apparently be subject, are those attributable to annual individual contributions. At maximum annual contributions over the past two decades of only $2,000 (up until IRA contributions limits were increased in 2002), an investor would have had to achieve rather phenomenal growth to actually accumulate more than $1 million solely attributable to such contributions. In addition, BAPCPA's changes allow for the courts to increase the $1 million IRA exemption limit in cases where it is in the "interests of justice" to do so. It remains for the courts to actually apply this provision of the law to show what might actually constitute such a need, but Congress made flexibility available to the courts if they are inclined to use it.

Caution

The above protection is a bankruptcy statute that protects assets in bankruptcy. But you can also get sued and not declare bankruptcy. This is then an issue of creditor protection and your IRA is still fully exposed (unless your state provides protection) to non-bankruptcy credit claims.

Before you take distributions or rollover opportunities, review retirement account for Company Stock in plan, look for NUA possibilities!

IRA Misfortune 101

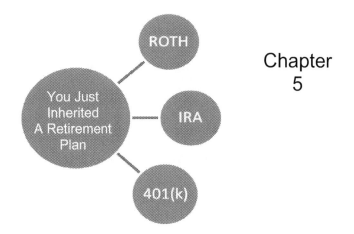

Chapter 5

Action Items......

You inherit an IRA, What do you do?

Here are the steps, and we'll discuss them in order of priority:

- Review retirement plan of deceased, inspect for company stock, review net unrealized appreciation (NUA) opportunities. *(Chapter 1)*

- Separate your portion from other IRA beneficiaries.

- Re-title the IRA.

- Name a beneficiary.

- Move inherited IRA to the financial institution of your preference (if permitted by existing custodian).

- Invest the funds pursuant to your investment plan, a review of assets which can and cannot be placed in an IRA. (covered in Chapter 2)

- Complete a distribution form for each IRA with the current or new custodian for annual distributions in accordance with the required minimum distributions for beneficiaries. Update each year.

- Be ready to be contacted by the executor or trustee of the decedent's trust—you might owe estate taxes.

Review retirement plan of deceased

Inspect the plan for company stock, review net unrealized appreciation (NUA) opportunities. *(Chapter 1)*

This is a complicated area; please talk with your tax professional or a qualified IRA advisor about this issue.

Separate your portion from other IRA beneficiaries

Find out from the executor or trustee of the deceased where the IRA resides and get a copy of the beneficiary form if possible, death certificate, and affidavit of domicile. Present this to the custodian with your identification. Know what you want the custodian to do. Do you want to leave this IRA at this institution or do you want to move it? If you want to move it, then you will need to have established your new IRA at another institution and initiated their transfer process.

Re-title the IRA

It's likely that you want to establish the inherited IRA at the existing institution (remember the correct titling discussed earlier), and an IRA at your new custodian with the exact title. The title will be of this format: Mike Jones IRA (deceased January 10, 2004) F/B/O (for benefit of), Sally Jones. Once the titles match, the new custodian can transfer the IRA. **Remember:** *YOU CAN DO A DIRECT ROLLOVER (Trustee-to -Trustee Transfer) ON AN INHERITED IRA—DO NOT ACCEPT A CHECK FROM THE DECEDENT'S CUSTODIAN AND DELIVER IT TO YOUR CUSTODIAN. THIS WILL RENDER YOUR INHERITED IRA TAXABLE.*

Name a beneficiary

Think through your beneficiary selections carefully, and if undecided, do not leave this option blank. Pick at least one person, (any person, me if you like) and name that person as beneficiary.

Move it to the location you desire (if permitted by the existing custodian)

When you move an IRA from one custodian to another, you initiate the "trustee-to-trustee" transfer with a form from the accepting custodian. Just make sure that the titles of the IRA you want to transfer, and the title of the new IRA match if you want things to go smoothly. If you're not sure that you'll be with your new custodian permanently, check the custodian's rules to make sure you can transfer again later without restriction.

Invest the funds per your investment plan, keeping in mind the review of assets which should and should not be placed in an IRA covered earlier in the book

Complete a distribution form with your new custodian for annual distributions in accordance with the required minimum distributions for beneficiaries (remember to update each year).

Each year, you divide the prior year December 31 IRA balance by a divisor. The divisor is the denominator you get from the table in Publication 590 for beneficiaries (see chapter 3) in the year of death, and each year, you subtract one. Your first distribution is the year after the year of death

Note: it's possible that the deceased, if required to take mandatory distributions (i.e. was age 70½ or older) did not take their distribution in the year of death. He or she may have had other things on the mind. Ask. If that's the case, you'll need to take your share of the decedent's distribution and pay tax.

Be ready to be contacted by the executor or trustee of the decedent's trust—you might owe estate taxes.

If the decedent's estate is subject to estate tax (which does not need to be paid until nine months after death), you may get a call that you must pony up some taxes. Don't complain. You got a free IRA didn't you? If you don't have the cash from other sources, (MEMORY RECALL: Opportunity Costs) seek the advise of a professional advisor as to what would be the best strategy to implement for you.

If You're a Spouse Beneficiary

The spouse has more options than a non-spouse beneficiary. Here are the four options:

- You can rollover the decedent's IRA to your own. This is a good option if you are younger than the deceased, and can further delay the required beginning date for distributions. It's also a good option if you are past age 59½, so if you do take money from the IRA once its rolled over, there will be no penalty.

- You can do nothing. You can leave the IRA as is because the option above has no time limit. You can rollover the decedent's IRA to your name at any time. Please note, that distributions of the IRA, if left in the decedent's name, will need to occur on the same schedule as if the deceased were alive.

- You can re-file the IRA as an inherited IRA. This is a good option if you are younger than 59½ but need to make distributions from the account. Since beneficiaries never pay an early withdrawal penalty regardless of age, if you remain in the status of beneficiary, you can take distributions without penalty. You will of course need to take mandatory distributions as a beneficiary using the IRA table for beneficiaries. Each year you use the prior year, December 31 IRA balance and divide by the divisor from the table. Each year you consult the table for the new divisor that matches your current age.

- You can disclaim the inheritance. Any beneficiary can disclaim the inheritance but few often do, if not a spouse. Why would a spouse do this? Let's examine the scenario:

Disclaim Retirement Plan Money

When people set up beneficiaries for their IRAs, they don't know what the future holds. Assume a simple situation where the IRA owner has two heirs—a spouse and a child. The IRA owner names a spouse as the primary beneficiary and their child as the contingent beneficiary. However, this may not be good if years later, the family is wealthy and they seek ways to reduce their estate and accompanying estate taxes. Leaving the IRA to the spouse turns out to have been a bad idea—it would have been better to leave the IRA to the child and take advantage of the unified credit (the estate exemption).

Here's where the disclaimer comes in. The spouse who has been named as primary beneficiary disclaims the inheritance. It will now pass to the next in line as named by the deceased (the contingent beneficiary). The IRA will pass to the child and accomplish exactly what was desired but could not have been planned years before. The disclaimer is a beautiful thing when estate tax issues are concerned.

IRA Misfortune 101

Communication Point:

- The disclaimer must be made before the property is accepted. The beneficiary cannot have placed his or her name on the account or changed investments.

- The disclaimer is required within nine months of date of death.

- The potential to use the disclaimer must be well thought out in advance, when the IRA distribution is being planned, because it's easy to have a disclaimer that will not be qualified. A qualified disclaimer must pass to someone other than the disclaim ant, and without direction by the disclaim ant.

For example, if the property is disclaimed in favor of a trust to which the disclaim ant is the beneficiary, the property in effect goes back to the disclaim ant and that won't be a qualified disclaimer. There is an exception when the disclaim ant is the spouse. Or, if the property is being disclaimed in favor of a trust for which the disclaim ant is trustee. The trustee can direct disposition of the assets and again, the disclaimer will fail to be qualified.

Conclusion

If this does not seem confusing and overwhelming, you're a genius for insane information, a Certified Public Accountant or an expert Retirement Distribution Professional. Believe it or not, competently trained advisors understand all of this and to them, it all seems structured and logical. That's what happens after years of studying the tax code—it takes on a logic all of its own that actually seems to make sense.

We welcome your inquiries and invite you to visit our website:

www.IRARippleEffect.com

IRA Misfortune 101

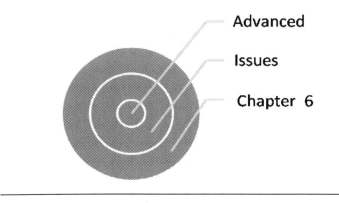

Advanced

Issues

Chapter 6

(Please see a Qualified advisor about the issues in this Section)

Divorce

Given the rate of divorce, it's critical to address how your retirement assets get handled. The question is "does your spouse have an interest in your retirement account?" Since the issues of marital property are governed by state law, you can only get a definitive answer from a divorce attorney in your state.
The answer, however, is probably that your spouse does have an interest in your account. There is only one instance where the answer could be that your spouse has no interest—in the case where you brought into marriage a retirement plan and made no further contributions during marriage. You then have a foundation to claim that the original assets are your separate pre-marital property, but the growth of the assets during the marriage will likely be deemed part-owned by your spouse.

An IRA or qualified plan interest may very well constitute a community asset. If so, the spouse (the non-participant spouse) of the IRA or qualified plan owner may be able to dispose of that interest on the death of the non-participant spouse. If the qualified plan is subject to ERISA,[9] federal law will preempt the spouse's power of testamentary disposition."

9

The Employee Retirement Income Security Act of 1974, 29 U.S.C. §1001, et seq., as amended. *"Boggs* v. *Boggs,* 117 S.Ct. 1754, 138 L.Ed.2d 45, 65 U.S. L.W. 4418(1997).

IRA Misfortune 101

Most employer plans are ERISA plans and you must name your spouse as your beneficiary unless the spouse waives beneficiary status in writing. ERISA ordinarily will not apply to an IRA, even a rollover IRA, though the Supreme Court has yet to address this issue specifically. Therefore, most attorneys believe that the non-participant's community property interest in the participant's IRA will pass to the beneficiaries of the non-participant spouse at the spouse's death, in accordance with the non-participant's will if there is one, or under the laws of intestate distribution if there is no will. However, during your lifetime, your accounts are subject to risks of divorce.

"Wait a minute," you protest, *"I earned that money and only my name is on it. That's not fair."* If you think life is fair, you're too young to be reading this book. This is money earned during the marriage and is therefore considered a community asset by your spouse's attorney.

If you are splitting or transferring an IRA, the divorce agreement will be the controlling document. Your divorce settlement will include this language, *"Any division of property accomplished or facilitated by any transfer of IRA or SEP account funds from one spouse or ex-spouse to the other is deemed to be made pursuant to this divorce settlement and is intended to be tax-free under Section 408(d)(6) of the Internal Revenue Code."*

There are five ways IRA money can get transferred incident to a divorce settlement :

1. The IRA may be continued and the name of the owner changed (in the case where the entire IRA is being transferred to the spouse).

2. A trustee-to-trustee transfer to a new or existing IRA is completed.

3. If a partial transfer is made, the portion being retained is transferred to a new IRA and the name is changed on the old IRA to the spouse

4. Funds are withdrawn and transferred subject to the 60 day rollover rules to the spouses new or existing IRA.

5. An IRA distribution is made and given to the spouse who completed the 60-day rollover.

Funds received from an IRA due to a divorce agreement must remain in an IRA until age 59½ or they will be subject to penalty.

If you divorce with money in a qualified plan, it will get split subject to a Qualified Domestic Relations Order (QDRO). Regarding the 10% penalty for people under age 59½, funds received subject to a QDRO are exempt.

Note that if you have a "do-it-yourself divorce, you do not want to tell your employer to transfer part of your plan to your spouse. Doing so without a properly drafted QDRO is a taxable distribution to you (and tax free cash to your spouse). So be sure to have a QDRO drafted which contains:

• Name and mailing address of the "plan participant" (you) and the "alternate payee" (your ex);

• Each retirement qualified plan account to be split under your divorce;

• The dollar amount or percentage of benefits to be paid from each account to the alternate payee; and

• The number of payments or benefits period covered by the QDRO.

Your papers should also specify that a qualified domestic relations order is being established under your state's domestic relations laws and Section 414(p) of the Internal Revenue Code.

- The dollar amount or percentage of benefits to be paid from each account to the alternate payee; and

- The number of payments or benefits period covered by the QDRO.

Your papers should also specify that a qualified domestic relations order is being established under your state's domestic relations laws and Section 414(p) of the Internal Revenue Code.

Exceptions to the 70½ Rule

If you work for a company and do not own at least 5% of the company, you don't need to take distributions until April 1 of the year after you retire, regardless of your age. You can even be working part time. This exception applies only to the plan of the company for which you currently work. It does not apply to your IRA or to money you have left in plans of ex-employers.

If you have a 403b plan, you may delay distributions of contributions you made prior to 1987 until you reach age 75. You will need to withdraw post-1986 contributions based on the normal age 70½ rule.

Note: You can be make contributions to a retirement plan while you may be distributing from others. You can make contributions to a Roth IRA (if you have earned income) past age 70½, or you can make contributions to your employers 401(k) if working or your own Keogh plan if operating a business.

The Pro Rata Rule

It's not uncommon that people can have both pre-tax dollars and post-tax dollars in their IRAs or qualified plans. This happened under the following circumstances:

Qualified plans allowed non-deductible contributions (i.e. the employee's contributions had already been taxed). IRS rules allows contributions to IRAs that may not be tax deductible. Since these funds have already been taxed, you don't want to pay tax on them again when you distribute them. With regard to your IRA, it's your job to keep track of these already taxed amounts (IRS provides form 8606). If you have lost this form or failed to keep track, the folks at IRS will probably not get upset. If you cannot show the amounts on which you have already paid tax, you will pay tax on them again and you probably won't get a notice from the IRS for this error.

Regarding your employer's plan, most employers keep track of these amounts and report them to you when you retire. The good news here is that these are post-tax funds you can take at retirement and use as you desire, as you have already paid tax. You need not roll them to an IRA but are permitted to do so and enjoy further tax deferred potential growth.

Note: You can take out all of your after-tax contributions, tax-free, before rolling your qualified plan dollars to an IRA. Pay attention to the word "before."

Before you complete a rollover, consider if you will need the money soon. If so, it probably won't pay to rollover the after -tax money to an IRA. This is because once you roll over after-tax money to an IRA, you cannot withdraw it tax-free. The after -tax funds become part of the IRA and any withdrawals from the IRA are subject to the "Pro Rata Rule."

The Pro Rata Rule requires that each distribution from an IRA contain a proportionate amount of both the taxable and the nontaxable amounts in the account. The non-taxable amounts are called "basis." In an IRA, basis is the amount of non-deductible contributions made to the IRA.

IRA Misfortune 101

Example

>   Molly has $100,000 in an IRA, $20,000 is the basis
> (the total of her non-deductible contributions made over
> the years). She rolls over $200,000 from her former
> employer's plan to the IRA, of which $10,000 is from
> after-tax contributions. After the rollover, she will have
> $300,000 in her IRA. The basis becomes $30,000 (the
> $20,000 non-deductible plus the $10,000 of after-tax
> funds rolled into the IRA = $30,000 basis).

>   Molly has decided to withdraw $10,000 of after-tax
> money from the rejuvenated IRA, figuring it will all be
> tax-free. **It won't be**. Only $1,000 of the withdrawal
> will be tax-free. She will have to pay tax on the other
> $9,000. The Pro Rata Rule requires that each withdrawal
> contain a proportionate amount of both taxable and non-
> taxable funds. Therefore, the non-taxable amount in the
> IRA is $30,000 and that is 10% of the total $300,000 IRA
> balance after the rollover. This means that each with-
> drawal will be 10% tax-free and 90% taxable.

>   Another option is to convert Molly's entire
> $300,000 IRA to a Roth IRA (assuming she otherwise
> qualifies for the conversion). Then all withdrawals will
> be tax-free. She'll pay tax on $270,000; the $30,000 of ba-
> sis will transfer tax-free to the Roth IRA. A partial   con-
> version would require the use of the Pro Rata Rule.

Exceptions to the 10% Penalty

Previously, we discussed Section 72(t) and the ability to remove funds from an IRA before age 59½ using substantial equal   periodic payments. There are other ways to avoid the 10% penalty, and here is a list.

IRC Section 72(t) penalty exemption	Major Restrictions
Distribution due to the disability of a participant.	- Participant must be disabled within the meaning of IRC section 72(m)(7).
Distribution as part of a series of substantially equal periodic payments.	- Payments must not occur less frequently than annually. - Payments from plans other than IRAs or individual retirement annuities must not begin before employee separates from service.
Distribution due to separation from service.	- Does not apply if the separation from service occurs before the year the participant turns 55. - Does not apply to IRA distributions or to self-employed individuals.
Distribution less than or equal to deductible medical expenses.	- Does not apply to pre-1997 IRA distributions.
Distribution to unemployed participant for health insurance premiums.	- Applies only to IRA distributions. - Participant must have received federal or state unemployment compensation for 12 consecutive weeks or have qualified under the self-employment provision. - Limited to amount of health insurance premiums paid.
Distribution for qualified higher education expenses of the participant or spouse, or their children or grandchildren.	-Applies only to IRA distributions. - Does not apply if participant qualifies for another exemption.
Distribution for the first-time purchase of a principal residence by the participant or spouse, or their child or grandchild.	-Applies only to IRA distributions. - Distribution must be used within 120 days to pay qualified acquisition costs. Lifetime limit of $10,000. Does not apply if participant qualifies for another exemption.

IRA Misfortune 101

Distribution subject to loan agreement.	- Loan agreement must be legally enforceable. - Term of loan cannot exceed five years unless distribution is used to acquire a principal residence. - Participant must adhere to specified repayment schedule and the amount of the loan is limited.
Distribution made to a beneficiary or the estate of a participant on or after the participant's death.	- Only applies to spousal beneficiary if spouse elects to leave plan assets in participant's name rather than rolling them over into IRA established in spouse's own name.
Dividend distribution to ESOP participant.	- Distribution must meet conditions for dividend deductibility established in IRC section 402(e)(1)(A).
Distribution pursuant to federal tax levy on plan under section 6631.	- Does not apply to pre-2000 distributions or distributions used to pay federal income taxes in the absence of a levy under IRC section 6631.
Distribution to alternate payee under a qualified domestic relations order.	-Does not apply to IRA distributions. -Applies to reduced annuity payment regardless of age retiree makes election and retires.
Distribution to federal retiree electing lump sum credit and reduced annuity.	- Does not apply to lump-sum distribution if retiree makes the election and retires before the year he or she reaches age 55.
Distribution rolled over into another qualified retirement plan within 60 days of the distribution.	- IRS can waive the 60-day rollover period if it believes the participant missed the deadline because of a "hardship" beyond his or her control.
Distribution to correct excess contributions.	- Applies to 402(g), 401 (k), and 401 (m) plans and IRAs.
Distribution upon conversion from traditional to Roth IRA.	- Applies to entire distribution (including portion of distribution includable in income).

Deducting an IRA Loss

Being able to claim a loss on your IRA does not necessarily mean you will be able to actually deduct that loss in regards to your taxes. There are still additional stumbling blocks.

The loss cannot be claimed if you take the standard deduction. The loss can only be claimed as a miscellaneous itemized deduction subject to the 2% of adjusted gross income (AGI) limitation. The loss on an IRA or Roth IRA is included in that total. If the loss is large enough, it will be more advantageous to itemize deductions rather than using the standard deduction.

If this barrier is passed and your 2008 AGI (Adjusted Gross Income) limits, (2008 it was $159,950, married filing joint, $79,975 for those filing married-separate), part of the deduction can be further limited.

Don't forget about the AMT (Alternative Minimum Tax), all of the 2% miscellaneous. itemized deductions are lost. Yes, including any deduction you were hoping for, on this IRA loss.

IF MY IRA IS LESS THAN MY TOTAL CONTRIBUTIONS, CAN I DEDUCT THE $12, 250 LOSS?

Rebecca, a wonderfully young person at heart and just turned 60 this year, has only had one traditional IRA. She has made the maximum contributions, including catch up contributions (totaling $81,500) since the start of the IRA at age 26 in 1975. She is an engineer and had assembled all the IRA contribution data for our review (see contribution chart). Just five years ago she had an account value of $220,000. Since than, her IRA value has dropped and now she is a little apprehensive in opening up her statements. Today (2009) her account has declined to $69,250. This represents $12,250 less than her deductible contributions. Over the years, Rebecca made

ZERO non-deductable traditional IRA contributions, so her loss of IRA account value is non-deductible. If Rebecca had some non-deductible contributions and had withdrawn or transferred the traditional IRA portion, she could assess the loss on the non-deductible portion.

Communication Point: Publication 590 Summary

1.) **Must itemize deductions, loss claimed as miscellaneous itemized deduction, must exceed 2% AGI, including other itemized deductions.**
2.) **Must have basis (non-deductible contributions). Don't forget about those funds transferred or contributed to a Roth; they all have basis.**
3.) **Withdraw all IRAs leaving basis in plan.**
4.) **The amount of the basis must exceed the amount withdrawn.**
5.) **Review Alternative Minimum Tax (AMT) rules The loss deduction will vanish if subject to AMT.**

History of Rebecca's IRA Contributions per Year

Contribution Years	Amount Contributed for these Years
1975—1981	$1, 500.00
1982—2001	$2,000.00
2002—2004	$3,500.00
2005	$4,500.00
2006—2007	$5,000.00
2008	$6,000.00

ATTENTION 70½ AND OVER
No Required Minimum Distributions for 2009

Our office is getting calls every day regarding the suspension of Required Minimum Distributions (RMD). While it is true, that one of the provisions in the Worker, Retiree, and Employer Recovery Act of 2008 (WRERA) has given retires the ability to suspend RMDs for 2009. Consider a look at the facts, and one of those calls we received.

A $250,000 IRA....Jerry, (the lower the tax maniac) has reviewed the 2009 WRERA, and believes this is such a huge opportunity for his IRA account to recover some of its loss, and at the same time lower his tax for 2009. Table 6.1 (pg 144) shows estimated RMDs for Jerry for the next 15 years; his age in 2009 is age 74. The growth he wants to use on this asset is 6% annually. Table 6.2 (pg 142) is the same information except with Jerry taking advantage of WRERA and delaying the RMDs for 2009.

As you review these tables, the distribution totals appear to equal each other after just 15 years. While most assume that this RMD gift will save them taxes, it will in fact, raise RMD annual distributions in the future, should account values elevate to previous levels. The tax difference, assuming the money is distributed at a 25% tax bracket, is $307.25. If congress decides to increase Jerry's taxes by just 10% (35% bracket), his tax difference will reverse and the delay in RMD distributions will actually cost Jerry an additional $620.25 over the 15 years. When you apply opportunity cost, the difference moves into the thousands.

Let's cover some other RMD issues.

So now you have completed your due diligence, and have decided to delay 2009 RMD, but the IRA custodian is sending you monthly checks already, and you have received six so far in 2009.

What can you do?

You or your spouse can roll funds back to your IRA within 60 days of distribution, and stop the reaming distribution for 2009. A non-spouse beneficiary is unable to make this   transaction because they are not allowed to do a 60 day rollover.

RMDs resume normal distribution unless congress in 2009 assembles another RMD change. As reviewed earlier in a recent case, the balance may be larger and you are a year older, so the distribution will most likely be higher than the 2009 RMD would have been.

Many of the charities are having contribution problems for 2009. Many of the wealthier owners of retirement plans were transferring their RMDs to a favorite charity. The Qualified Charitable Distribution (QCD) provision, which is still effective for tax year 2009, allows the taxpayer to transfer RMDs to his charity and escape taxation on the distribution. Since this law went into effect, and RMDs are not required for 2009, they are seeing these donations decline year-to-date for 2009.

One of our callers said his RMDs are $69,900 for 2009, and he wants to suspend this distribution, but will need to make a $5,000 withdrawal from his IRA. The suspension will not limit your access to your retirement account; triggering a withdrawal does not disturb his $69,900 suspended RMD.

As far as Roth IRA owners, they are not subject to RMDs, However non-spouse Roth IRA beneficiaries must take RMDs when they inherit, and yes, it's tax-free. The good news is, the new law allows RMDs from inherited Roth IRAs to also be waived for 2009. If the Roth IRA beneficiary is a spouse who rolled the Roth IRA over to his or her own Roth IRA, then that spouse is treated as the Roth IRA owner (in other words, as if he/she contributed all of the money to their own Roth IRA), and is never required to take lifetime distributions, the same as any Roth IRA owner. So the suspension of 2009 RMDs does not apply since the surviving spouse is not an issue to RMDs in this case.

We continue to see taxpayers giving the church $3,000 and not enough limited deduction to write off the donation. At the same time their RMDs are $3,000 and fully taxable. This is a no brainer. Keep the liquid money and transfer the RMDs to their charity, therefore, eliminating the tax.

Table 6.1
Normal Distributions

Age	Normal RMD Distributions
74	10,504
75	11,100
76	11,728
77	12,331
78	13,025
79	13,685
80	14,373
81	15,090
82	15,835
83	16,609
84	17,411
85	18,117
86	18,835
87	19,561
88	20,291
Distribution Total	$228,495

Table 6.2
Delay Distributions for 2009

Age	Normal RMD Distributions
74	0.00
75	11,572
76	12,227
77	12,856
78	13,579
79	14,267
80	14,985
81	15,732
82	16,509
83	17,315
84	18,152
85	18,888
86	19,636
87	20,393
88	21,155
Distribution Total	$227,265

APPENDIX 1:
QUESTIONS AND
ANSWERS

Can I do a rollover from my employer's plan to a Roth IRA?

The IRS will tell you, YES you can. HOWEVER, Your Plan Administrator may tell you NO. Don't panic, you must first do a rollover to a traditional IRA and then to a Roth IRA.

What items cannot be rolled over to an IRA?

The required mandatory distribution

72(t) Distributions

Inherited IRAs to non-spouse beneficiaries, Trustee to Trustee transfer is allowed

What is a conduit IRA?

It is an IRA in which you keep segregated funds in order to retain their tax attributes. For example, if you are eligible for ten year averaging on distribution from a qualified plan, but choose to roll your qualified plan to an IRA and you keep that IRA separate from all other IRA accounts (thus, a conduit IRA), you may later roll those funds back to a qualified plan and exercise the ten year averaging option.

Can I pledge my IRA as collateral for a loan?

No. Pledging your IRA as collateral constitutes a distribution of the IRA, making it taxable (and subject to penalties if under age 59 ½). You can use your IRA to get a non-recourse loan to purchase some real estate. Your loan guarantor cannot be personally responsible for the loan.

What's a prohibited transaction?

The following are examples of prohibited transactions with respect to a traditional IRA

- *Borrowing money from it.*
- *Selling property to it.*
- *Receiving unreasonable compensation for managing it.*
- *Using it as security for a loan.*
- *Buying property for personal use (present or future).*

Do I have to take the Required Minimum Distributions (RMDs) if I am still working for the company that I am a part owner?

Still working at 70½ , at a company where you are more than 5% owner, does require distributions from the SEP-IRA and the 401K plan. SEP-IRA, and the 401k are considered employer plans. You can continue to add the maximum contribution to that 401k. Any contributions to a SEP IRA if you remain more than a 5% owner are allowed. If you were less than 5% owner you could delay distribution on the plan of the company where you are employed, but other retirement plans like an IRA would require RMDs.

APPENDIX 2: EXHIBITS

UNIFIED ESTATE AND GIFT TAXES

Amount Subject To Taxes	But not over	Rate of Tax
$ 00.00	$10,000	18%
$10,001	$20,000	20%
$20,001	$40,000	22%
$40,001	$60,000	24%
$60,001	$80,000	26%
$80,001	$100,000	28%
$100,001	$150,000	30%
$150,001	$250,000	32%
$250,001	$500,000	34%
$500,001	$750,000	37%
$750,001	$1,000,000	39%
$1,000,001	$1,250,000	41%
$1,250,001	$1,500,000	43%
$1,500,001	$2,000,000	45%
$2,000,001	$3,500,000	45%
$3,500,001	OVER	45%

Subject to unified tax credit per table below to U.S. citizens and residents. *GENERATION-SKIPPING* taxes may also apply.

IRA Misfortune 101

Tax Brackets for 2009

Taxable income (i.e. income minus deductions and exemptions) between:

Married, Joint

$0-$16,700	10%
$16,701-$67,900	15%
$67,901-$137,050	25%
$137,051-$208,850	28%
$208,851-$372,950	33%
over $372,950	35%

Single

$0-$8,350	10%
$8,351-$33,950	15%
$33,951-$82,250	25%
$82,251-$171,550	28%
$171,551-$372,950	33%
over $372,950	35%

Married, Separate

$0-$8,350	10%
$8,351-$33,950	15%
$33,951-$68,525	25%
$68,526-$104,425	28%
$104,426-$186,475	33%
over $186,475	35%

Head of Household

$0-$11,950	10%
$11,951-$45,500	15%
$45,501-$117,450	25%
$117,451-$190,200	28%
$190,201-$372,950	33%
over $372,950	35%

Estates and Trusts

$0-$2,300	15%
$2,301-$5,350	25%
$5,351-$8,200	28%
$8,201-$11,150	33%
over $11,150	35%

Corporations

$0-$50,000	15%
$50,001-$75,000	25%
$75,001-$100,000	34%
$100,001-$335,000	39%
$335,001-$18,333,333	34-38%
over $18,333,333	35%

IRA & Pension Plan Limits

IRA contribution
- Under age 50 — $5,000
- Age 50 and over — $6,000

Phaseout for deducting IRA contribution
- Married, joint — $89,000-$109,000 AGI
- Single, HOH[1] — $55,000-$65,000 AGI
- Married, separate — $0-$10,000 AGI

Phaseout for deducting spousal IRA
$166,000-$176,000 AGI

Phaseout of Roth contribution eligibility
- Married, joint — $166,000-$176,000 MAGI
- Single, HOH[1] — $105,000-$120,000 MAGI
- Married, separate — $0-$10,000 MAGI
- No Roth conversion if $100,000[3] MAGI

SEP contribution
- Up to 25% of compensation, limit $49,000

Compensation to participate in SEP — $550

SIMPLE elective deferral
- Under age 50 — $11,500
- Age 50 and over — $14,000

401(k), 403(b)[2], 457 and SARSEP elective
deferral under age 50 — $16,500

401(k), 403(b)[2], 457[3] and SARSEP elective
deferral age 50 and over — $22,000

Annual defined contribution limit — $49,000

Annual defined benefit limit — $195,000

Highly compensated employee — $110,000

Key Employee in top heavy plans
makes — $160,000

Annual compensation taken into account for
qualified plans — $245,000

Retirement Tax Credit
A percent tax credit for an IRA, 401(k), 403(b)
or 457 plan contribution, in addition to
deduction or exclusion, if
- Married, joint — Below $55,500 MAGI
- Head of household — Below $41,625 MAGI
- Single; Married, separate — Below $27,750 MAGI

1. Head of Household

2. Special increased limit may apply to certain 403(b)
contributors with 15 or more years of service

157

What is YOUR Social Security Retirement Age Timetable

Year of Birth Retired Workers	Retirement Age Full Benefits	Reached In
Before 1938	65	Before 2003
Born 1938	65 & 2 months	2003 & 2004
Born 1939	65 & 4 months	2004 & 2005
Born 1940	65 & 6 months	2005 & 2006
Born 1941	65 & 8 months	2006 & 2007
Born 1942	65 & 10 months	2007 & 2008
Born 1943 thru 1954	66	2009 thru 2020
Born 1955	66 & 2 months	2021 & 2022
Born 1956	66 & 4 months	2022 & 2023
Born 1957	66 & 6 months	2023 & 2024
Born 1958	66 & 8 months	2024 & 2025
Born 1959	66 & 10 months	2025 & 2026
Born 1960 & later	67	2027 and later

Reduction in S.S. Benefits To Carry On Working

Reduction in Social Security benefits do to work earnings	2009 Exempt amount if you earn more than	Earnings above exempt income reduce Social Security distribution by:
Before year in which worker reaches full retirement age	$13,560	Half or 50% Loosing $1 for every $2 earned
The months before birthday in year of which worker reaches full retirement age	$36,120	One Third or 33% Loosing $1 for every $3 earned
Month in which worker reaches full retirement age	All earnings exempt	Zero Or 0%

Social Security NOTES and FYI

Maximum Earnings (during work years) subject to FICA Tax:	**$106,800**

Income Brackets (in retirement) which cause Social Security benefits to be taxable		
Married Filing Joint (MAGI = Minimum Adjusted Gross Income)	**50% taxable**	**$32,000 MAGI**
	85% taxable	**$44,000 MAGI**
Single (MAGI = Minimum Adjusted Gross Income)	**50% taxable**	**$25,000 MAGI**
	85% taxable	**$34,000 MAGI**

Loss of social security retirement benefits in years prior to full retirement age, $1 in benefits will be lost for every $2 of earnings in excess of $14,160. In the year of full retirement age $1 in benefits will be lost for every $3 of earnings in excess of $37,680 (applies only to months of earnings prior to full retirement age). There is no limit on earnings beginning the month the individual attains full retirement age.

2009 Retirement Calendar

January 31: *Deadline for reporting:*

1. 2008 SIMPLE IRA contributions to account holders.
2. December 31,2008 IRA fair market values to account holders
3. 2008 IRA distributions to account holders on Form 1099-R
4. 2008 ESA distributions to recipients on Form 1099-Q
5. 2008 HSA distributions to recipients on Form 1099-SA
6. Sending 2008 RMD information to Traditional, SEP, and SIMPLE IRA owners who are age 70½ or older in 2009

February 28: *Deadline for reporting:*

Paper or magnetic media filers to send 2008 Forms 1099-R, 1099-Q, and 1099-SA to the IRS

March 17: *Normal Deadline:*

For calendar-year corporations to make SEP contributions and Employer non-elective or matching SIMPLE IRA contributions for 2008

March 31: *Deadline for reporting*

Deadline for electronic filers to send 2008 Forms 1099-R, 1099-Q,and 1099-SA to the IRS

April 1: *Deadline for reporting*

Deadline for paying the 2008 RMD to Traditional, SEP, and SIMPLE IRA owners who attained 70½ in 2008

April 15: *Normal Deadline*

1. For Traditional IRA, Roth IRA, or ESA for 2008 contributions
2. For calendar-year unincorporated businesses to make SEP contributions

April 30: *Deadline for reporting*

ESA contributions to designated beneficiaries for 2008

May 31: *Deadline for*

Completing a corrective distribution of a 2008 ESA contribution to avoid an excess contribution

June 2: *Deadline for*

1. Forms 5498,5498-ESA, and 5498-SA to the IRS for 2008
2. 2008 Form 5498, information to Traditional, Roth, SEP, & SIMPLE IRA holders
3. 2008 Form 5498-SA information to HSA holders

October 1: *Deadline for*

A business to establish a SIMPLE IRA plan for 2008, unless:

1. The business is established after October 1,2008
2. The employer previously maintained a SIMPLE IRA plan

October 15: *Deadline for*

1. Recharacterizing 2008 ERA contributions and Roth IRA conversions
2. Completing a corrective distribution from an IRA for a contribution for 2008 for taxpayers who file their 2008 federal income tax return on a timely basis

November 1: *Deadline for*

Employers who are continuing to offer a SIMPLE IRA plan to send 2009 notification to eligible employees

December 31: *Deadline for*

1. Distributing an amount from a Traditional, SEP, or SIMPLE IRA for conversion to a Roth IRA to have the conversion taxable for 2009
2. Paying 2009 RMDs to Traditional IRA owners who attained age 70½ before 2009
3. Paying RMDs to beneficiaries who must take a death distribution for 2008

Extended listing of Table 1.2 Bank Failures for 2009 per FDIC Website 6/30/2009

Bank Name	CERT #	Closing Date
Mirae Bank, Los Angeles, CA	57332	26-Jun-09
MetroPacific Bank, Irvine, CA	57893	26-Jun-09
Horizon Bank, Pine City, MN	9744	26-Jun-09
Neighborhood Community Bank, Newnan, GA	35285	26-Jun-09
Community Bank/ West Georgia, Villa Rica, GA	57436	26-Jun-09
First National Bank of Anthony, Anthony, KS	4614	19-Jun-09
Cooperative Bank, Wilmington, NC	27837	19-Jun-09
Southern Community Bank, Fayetteville, GA	35251	19-Jun-09
Bank of Lincolnwood, Lincolnwood, IL	17309	5-Jun-09
Citizens National Bank, Macomb, IL	5757	22-May-09
Strategic Capital Bank, Champaign, IL	35175	22-May-09
BankUnited, FSB, Coral Gables, FL	32247	21-May-09
Westsound Bank, Bremerton, WA	34843	8-May-09
America West Bank, Layton, UT	35461	1-May-09
Citizens Community Bank, Ridgewood, NJ	57563	1-May-09
Silverton Bank, N.A., Atlanta, GA	26535	1-May-09
First Bank of Idaho, Ketchum, ID	34396	24-Apr-09
First Bank of Beverly Hills, Calabasas, CA	32069	24-Apr-09
Michigan Heritage Bank, Farmington Hills, MI	34369	24-Apr-09
American Southern Bank, Kennesaw, GA	57943	24-Apr-09
Great Basin Bank of Nevada, Elko, NV	33824	17-Apr-09
American Sterling Bank, Sugar Creek, MO	8266	17-Apr-09
New Frontier Bank, Greeley, CO	34881	10-Apr-09

Extended listing of Table 1.2 Bank Failures for 2009 per FDIC Website 6/30/2009 Cont'd

Bank Name	CERT #	Closing Date
Cape Fear Bank, Wilmington, NC	34639	10-Apr-09
Omni National Bank, Atlanta, GA	22238	27-Mar-09
TeamBank, National Association, Paola, KS	4754	20-Mar-09
Colorado National Bank,Colorado Springs, CO	18896	20-Mar-09
FirstCity Bank, Stockbridge, GA	18243	20-Mar-09
Freedom Bank of Georgia, Commerce, GA	57558	6-Mar-09
Security Savings Bank, Henderson, NV	34820	27-Feb-09
Heritage Community Bank, Glenwood, IL	20078	27-Feb-09
Silver Falls Bank, Silverton, OR	35399	20-Feb-09
Pinnacle Bank of Oregon, Beaverton, OR	57342	13-Feb-09
Corn Belt Bank and Trust Company, Pittsfield, IL	16500	13-Feb-09
Riverside Bank of the Gulf Coast, Cape Coral, FL	34563	13-Feb-09
Sherman County Bank, Loup City, NE	5431	13-Feb-09
County Bank, Merced, CA	22574	6-Feb-09
Alliance Bank, Culver City, CA	23124	6-Feb-09
FirstBank Financial Services, McDonough, GA	57017	6-Feb-09
Ocala National Bank, Ocala, FL	26538	30-Jan-09
Suburban Federal Savings Bank, Crofton, MD	30763	30-Jan-09
MagnetBank, Salt Lake City, UT	58001	30-Jan-09
1st Centennial Bank, Redlands, CA	33025	23-Jan-09
Bank of Clark County, Vancouver, WA	34959	16-Jan-09
National Bank of Commerce, Berkeley, IL	19733	16-Jan-09

IRA Misfortune 101

Bank Name	CERT #	Closing Date
Sanderson State Bank, Sanderson, TX	11568	12-Dec-2008
Haven Trust Bank , Duluth, GA	35379	12-Dec-2008
First Georgia Community Bank, Jackson, GA	34301	5-Dec-2008
PFF Bank and Trust, Pomona, CA	28344	21-Nov-2008
Downey Savings and Loan, Newport Beach, CA	30968	21-Nov-2008
The Community Bank, Loganville, GA	16490	21-Nov-2008
Security Pacific Bank, Los Angeles, CA	23595	7-Nov-2008
Franklin Bank, SSB, Houston, TX	26870	7-Nov-2008
Freedom Bank. Bradenton. FL	57930	31-Oct-2008
Alpha Bank & Trust. Alpharetta. GA	58241	31-Oct-2008
Meridian Bank. Eldred. IL	13789	10-Oct-2008
Main Street Bank. Northville. MI	57654	10-Oct-2008
Washington Mutual Bank. Henderson. NV and Washinaton Mutual Bank FSB, Park City. UT	32633	25-Sept-2008
Ameribank, Northfork, WV	6782	19-Sept-2008
Silver State Bank, Henderson, NV En Espanol	34194	5-Sept-2008
Integrity Bank, Alpharetta. GA	35469	29-Aug-2008
The Columbian Bank and Trust, Topeka. KS	22728	22-Aug-2008
First Priority Bank, Bradenton, FL	22728	22-Aug-2008
First Heritaqe Bank, NA, Newport Beach. CA	57961	25-July-2008
First National Bank of Nevada, Reno, NV	27011	25-July-2008
IndyMac Bank, Pasadena, CA	29730	9-July-2008
First Integrity Bank, NA, Staples, MN	12736	30-May-2008

Bank Name	CERT #	Closing Date
ANB Financial, NA, Bentonville, AR	33901	9-May-2008
Hume Bank, Hume, MO	1971	7-Mar-2008
Douglass National Bank. Kansas City. MO	24660	25-Jan-2008
Miami Valley Bank. Lakeview. OH	16848	4-Oct-2007
NetBank, Alpharetta. GA	32575	28-Sept-2007
Metropolitan Savings Bank. Pittsburgh. PA	35353	2-Feb-2007
Bank of Ephraim. Ephraim. UT	1249	25-Jun-2004
Reliance Bank. White Plains. NY	26778	19-Mar-2004
Guaranty National Bank of Tallahassee, FL	26838	12-Mar-2004
Dollar Savings Bank, Newark, NJ	31330	14-Feb-2004
Pulaski Savinas Bank. Philadelphia. PA	31330	14-Feb-2004
The First National Bank of Blanchardville,WA	11639	9-May-2003
Southern Pacific Bank. Torrance. CA	11639	9-May-2003
The Farmers Bank of Cheneyville, LA	16445	17-Dec-2002
The Bank of Alamo. Alamo. TN	9961	8-Nov-2002
AmTrade Intnl Bank of Georgia, Atlanta, GA	33784	30-Sept-2002
Universal Federal Savings Bank, Chicago, IL	29355	27-Jun-2002
Connecticut Bank of Commerce. Stamford. CT	19183	26-Jun-2002
New Century Bank. Shelby Township. MI	34979	28-Mar-2002
Net 1st National Bank. Boca Raton. FL	26652	1-Mar-2002

IRA Misfortune 101

About The Author

TIM H. COOPER CRFA®, a Registered Investment Advisor, is well known for his use of technology to advance his clients economic world. A 27 experienced professional in building wealth for thousands of individuals. His use of the most advanced and technical methods in building toward cost-effective strategies that breaks through the rules the Financial Institutions want you to follow. His uncommon approach can help you move toward your independent lifestyle and economic freedom. He has lectured hundreds of financial advisors as well as many individuals who have attended his seminars. His clients become wealthy, successful and happy knowing the legal techniques to your advantage. Tim is the President of Creative Wealth Systems, a graduate of the University of Hard Knox training, lives in Westerville, Ohio father of four, Crystal, Tiffany, Tyler and Lacey, grandfather of six, Courtney, Kaylie, Cooper, Conner, Makala and Jackson.

To learn more visit :
WWW.IRARippleEffect.com